Heartfelt Emotions

Enjoy!

Christine Brownlee
(Roman)

Heartfelt Emotions

Lee Christine Brownlee

TATE PUBLISHING
AND ENTERPRISES, LLC

Published by Tate Publishing & Enterprises, LLC
127 E. Trade Center Terrace | Mustang, Oklahoma 73064 USA
1.888.361.9473 | www.tatepublishing.com

Tate Publishing is committed to excellence in the publishing industry. The company reflects the philosophy established by the founders, based on Psalm 68:11,
"The Lord gave the word and great was the company of those who published it."

Book design copyright © 2016 by Tate Publishing, LLC. All rights reserved.
Cover design by Albert Ceasar Compay
Interior design by Jomar Ouano

Published in the United States of America

ISBN: 978-1-68301-507-9
Poetry / General
16.07.01

To my family who has made my life complete and to my husband
who gave me his support before passing away from cancer in 2009.

ACKNOWLEDGMENTS

To everyone who support and encouraged me to continue writing.

To the survivors of cancer for their courage and faith to fight for survival, and the Armed Forces of the United States for their sacrifice and devotion to our country and protecting our freedom.

Last, but most importantly, God, for giving me this opportunity, skill and faith.

CONTENTS

MY PLEDGE TO OUR GREAT POETS

I, a humble poet,
Pledge to my forefathers of literature,
To honor their talent,
Their intelligence,
That I have been given.

I will always start each poem,
With a capital letter,
Punctuate when needed,
And end every sentence,
Or verse with a period.

I will not abuse or berate,
The knowledge I have taken,
From my predecessors,
But use the knowledge they have
Given me to recreate beauty,
Emotion, and literature,
To the best of my ability.

POETRY

Is an explosion of internal emotion,
Felt from your minutest brain area,
To the tip of your toes.

Comprised of love, hate, and fear,
Happiness, and sadness,
Tranquility, turbulence and bliss.

Spatial in size,
An odyssey of hope,
From a dismal past.

Anxiously awaits,
A new sequence of thought,
To expand and explore.

Creating beauty,
Or life's combative,
Past nightmares.

Fall in love or lust,
Whatever the tale brings,
Encasing you in its web.

Poetry is a dream come true,
Written and recorded,
A documented view of thought.

Lee Christine Brownlee

MY BEST FRIEND

Spoken with my best friend,
Shared my every thought.
He has always been there to listen,
No judgmental actions at all.

Think he never listens,
I've heard his gentle voice,
"That faux pas wasn't so bad,
You'll make a better choice."

Listening to my best friend,
He never turns me away,
I know his love and kindness
Is guiding me along the way.

My best and dearest friend is kind,
He's always waiting in the shadows,
To help me clearly understand my life,
He watches over me ... that's right!

Always feeling safe and loved,
No matter where I am.
Who, you ask, is my dearest friend?
Why, it's God!
Who else could care this much?

MADE MY RESERVATION

Saved my money, made my reservation,
I'm taking that train down Memory Lane.
While the train is moving down the tracks,
I'll be starting my trip back to Happiness.

The conductor called, "All aboard."
No luggage needed where I'm going.
Clickety-Clack, Clickety-Clack,
This train is on its way to Happiness Park.

Clickety-Clack, Clickety-Clack,
The motion of the train, swaying of the car,
Traveling back in time you see,
Where happiness was once my dream.

Clickety-Clack, mentally adrift, back in time,
We've stopped to watch my children play.
How joyous the days of faces with smiles.
Moments when life was carefree and gay.

Further back in time,
Remembering the love that once was.
Clickety-Clack, Clickety-Clack,
Days of happiness that promised.

Clickety-Clack, back in time,
Next stop, my wedding day,
A beautiful church along the way.
That was a happy day, so they say.

Lee Christine Brownlee

Clickety-Clack, Clickety-Clack
Start to plan my life, just the beginning.
We'll skip the rest of that day,
As we Clickety-Clack away.

The conductor yells, "Stay in your seats.
No stops till we reach our destination.
This is the train to Happiness."
Clickety-Clack, Clickety-Clack.

Now the conductor announces…
"We are minutes away from our last stop.
At Happiness Park, please disembark."
"Next stop will be our Final Stop."

Drift and dream of days gone by.
"Enjoy your stay in Happiness Park.
This train will return tomorrow,
To take you back to today."

Clickety-Clack, Clickety-Clack, Clickety-Clack…

THE ROSE

You are the rose of my life,
With every day that passes,
You blossom more beautifully,
With your petals everlasting.

Your shades of pastels increase in beauty,
While your growth never stops,
Inspiring me with your wisdom,
Constantly adding more beauty as you age.

You brighten every day,
With your personality,
Never fading, never wilting,
Forever and always blooming.

(Written for my daughter, Christine.)

LOVE ME TOMORROW?

Will you love me tomorrow,
The way you did yesterday?
Will you want me always near you,
The way I want you near me today?

Can we hold on to our emotions,
Until we're old and gray?
Sharing life's good times,
And hardships together along the way.

Will you miss me when I'm gone,
When my time on earth is over?
Can we hold on to this feeling,
Throughout the decades of life before us?

I will cherish our time together,
For as long as it will last.
If you will love me tomorrow,
The way you loved me in the past.

UNFINISHED LOVE AFFAIR

It's been so long since I've seen you.
Don't know how or why you stay,
At the forefront of my memory,
But you do and will always remain.

Time has passed, and the years have aged us.
What can replace the time we spent,
In our younger days?
Talking, dreaming, and planning a life.
Laughing and hoping as time passed us by,
Our friendship would be never-ending.

Well, the years have passed,
We have all gone our separate ways,
But the talks we had,
And the dreams we dreamed still linger today,
As unfinished dreams and incomplete endings.

The dreams we shared,
Still bring joyous tears when I think,
How time has slipped past.
But yet I see your face as I did then,
Beaming with life, smiling and carefree.

Those were the days of happy tears,
And unfinished love affairs.

CRUMBS FOR THE TAKING

Little pieces of my life crumble like stale bread.
Crumb-by-crumb I view little piles on the floor.
If I scoop the pieces of my life up,
Will it meld back together again,
Or will the crumbs be swept away,
In the trash like dust?

The crumbs are little pieces of my life,
My heart is broken into tiny pieces.
A puzzle never again is put back together,
As the pieces rearrange each time they tumble.

My life, a maze of crumbs.
A mosaic picture smashed to pieces.
When did it start to fall apart and crumble?
Will it last till the picture of life ends,
Or will life end before the picture crumbles?

My Heart Overflows

My heart renders love from lifetimes past,
Overflowing with emotion and tears.
Until my entire soul has emptied all it holds,
Into the world to be shared with all.

My inner love again renews and fills,
Over and over again for all to consume.
Such beauty that surrounds the earth,
Should be treasured and shared by all.

What motivates hate and greed to be spread,
Like a disease that kills all life.
Dissolves all emotion and feeling.
For the sake of covetousness and force.

Yet, my heart spills over with love,
Hoping to overpower the discontented.
Deluge them in glorious splendor,
Till they succumb to peace and contentment.

Out of Darkness

Lying on the beach,
My mind blank,
The bright star above drawing me nearer,
Slivers of darkness still appear,
But the never-ending brightness pulls me closer.

Is it a dream or is it the warmth of light?
Tugging at my heart to let go and follow.
Let go of the past and follow the light into the future,
Filled with warmth and new life.

This warm light bathes me in a calm,
With each breath I take.
Less pain, fewer worries, less stress.
While I cross over into absolute brilliance,
Of beauty beyond words.

Weakness dissipates and I'm overcome by strength.
Transformed into the setting of solace,
And the beauty of the distant light.
Is this my destiny or my dream?

Should I follow and go?
Or should I stay and awaken?
Disappearing into my solace,
Overwhelmed by desires for happiness.
Does life intensify sorrow,
Or enhance my desire for the hereafter?

THE DARK WOODS

The woods so dense,
So dark, so eerie.
Tree trunks thicker,
Than I remember.

Dampness hugs my throat,
And whispers cannot be heard.
But the rustling sound of branches,
I'll always recall,
The dreary, dense woods,
I'll always remember.

The shadowy figures pop in and out,
From behind tree trunks and limbs,
I remember sliver-like images,
They wait and watch,
While dusk looms around me.

Friend or foe I do not know,
Who is watching and who is hiding?
When dawn starts to trickle in above,
And darts through the tree trunks that surround me.
I will escape outside these woods,
To a safer place where I can be heard.

The woods so deep,
So dark, so eerie.
Will I last till dawn?
Or will the shadows devour me?

Lee Christine Brownlee

Subway Glance

My emotions run high,
When I see his face.
On the crowded subway,
During the morning rush.

Where is he coming from?
And where is he going?
These thoughts repeat,
In my head each morning.

He looks like a professional,
With an education.
Or am I staring at the worker,
Preparing for a day of labor?

Do I dare start a conversation,
With my dreamy subway guy?
Or if he glances my way,
Should I smile and say, "Hi"?

We are strangers on the train,
Endless mornings I stare and wait,
For just a hint of a smile,
From my dreamy subway guy.

HEARTBREAK

A heart breaks into many pieces,
The shattering can be heard from far away.
Either lack of love or loss of lover,
A shattered heart finds it hard to recover.

We will survive this internal damage,
But not without emotional scars.
The healing process takes time to mend,
All broken pieces that shattered within.

Be careful in meeting someone new,
There could be a broken heart there too,
Left by a previous lover, no doubt,
In need of your touch to mend that heart.

Lee Christine Brownlee

HOPES AND DREAMS

Twilight appears to cast shadows,
On a day's memories.
Encouraging our thoughts,
To stray beyond the edge.
Between the cracks of reality,
And imagination.

Resting in the crevices,
Of thoughts and wishes.
Hidden in the nooks and crannies,
Are dreams and hopes.
Reconstruction of past sentiment,
And angled cognitive process.

Bouncing from reality,
To imaginary thoughts,
Then perceptual cognition.
Testing our ability to decipher,
Genuine hopes and dreams,
From castles in the air.

MY LOVE

Over the rainbow,
And beneath the sea.
The depth and height,
Of my love for thee.

DEPTH

My heart sinks,
To the depth of the sea.
As my mind escapes,
From my dismal life.

My emotions run cold,
While my senses drain.
The delayed reaction,
To ever-taunting dreams.

Dreams that began,
The day I lost you.
What will become,
Of my memories,
When I'm through?

PACIFIC SUNSET

Daylight begins to fade — the sun has moved west for its daily descent,
Reflections of bright amber shining as the sun's voyage begins.
Sunset reflects the beauty in nature's eyes,
Vibrant colors intensify into deeper, more brilliant shades.
Lights exploding into vibrating hues of rich, glowing orange and reds,
Fading softly to many shades of pink.
Reflection of colors mirrored on the water's crest,
Blending into the sky, it begins to fade to darkness.
Breathtaking and exuberant causing your heart to race,
Watching the ocean swallow the sun whole,
'Til there is nothing but darkness to embrace.
The beauty seen watching the sun disappear,
Sitting on the seashore gazing in amazement,
Expecting to hear a sizzle.
As its glow decimates before your eyes,
This ball of fire extinguished by the ocean's water.
A final view of this sunset resembling colors on its surface of golden glory.
Mystic view of the sun slowly vanishing out of sight.
The ocean is calm, ripples of light exposing its crest.
End of daylight allowing luminance of the stars,
Light our way to a new day.
Thoughts move from the sunset to the constellation above us,
Glittering and sparkling — guide us through the night, bringing the joy
    of other lights.

NOTHINGNESS

You find yourself staring.
Not at an object,
But a blank canvas,
Or a sheet of blank paper,
Nothingness.

Your mind,
A blank screen.
Your thoughts?
None.
Just more nothingness.

Time has elapsed.
How much time?
We do not know.
Who was marking time?
Just marking...
Marking nothingness.

LOST MY GUY

Lost the one guy I found,
After searching all over town.
What will I do without him,
In my life alone night and day?

Lost the one guy I loved,
Who purified the air I breathe.
Held me tight in the moonlight,
While whispering, he'd always be mine.

Lost the one guy I needed so,
Who illuminated my every day.
There when dark clouds rolled in,
Throughout eternity.

Will keep searching till I find him,
Wherever he may be.
To draw him back into my life,
Tell me if you've seen him... Please....

Lee Christine Brownlee

HELD CAPTIVE

Caught in the vacuum of love.
Feel the pull of the suction.
Swirling round in your head.
Captured whole.

'Round and 'round in motion,
There's no way up or out.
The swirling feel inside,
Keeps pulling you into love.

Love captures your heart,
Strength and emotions.
Leaves you without,
An escape from within.

Give in and go with that swirl,
That pulls like an undertow in the sea.
Maybe this time will be different,
The depth of love that you're in.

BLUE ON BLUE

Sitting alone on the beach,
Lost in the memory of you.
Not concentrating on anything,
Just notice that I'm so blue.

Days of love and contentment?
Nothing new to report.
Recall your wonderful smile,
Just lost in the memory of you.

Transference

Happiness and sadness,
Transferred from others.
Blends, changes, or strengthens,
The emotions of many.

Poetry reverberates
In the minds of readers.
Displays harmony of words,
Noting life's joys and sadness.

Passed on by others their awareness,
Long lost loves and hates.
Fears and doubts,
Hoping for wisdom from above.

Forgiving for emotional losses,
Praying for new beginnings.
Dancing to the miracles in life,
And hoping for the existence of love.

Bereavement in death,
The exhilaration of new life.
Yet the joy of new-found friends,
Sharing life's experiences today.

Transference and sharing,
Awakens the spirit.
Unnerving the soul,
To recognize imposing threats.

Cognizance brings to the surface,
Awareness of our surroundings.
Lessens dubiety,
And strengthens reality.

And Liberty for All

Our nation's liberty remains stern and strong,
Though there are people who wish us to fall.
Our shields are the strength of our nation's force,
And the will of the people will never default.

Composed of people from every nation,
Building together a nation of prosperity.
Our nation was, and is created by many,
Teaching us of her sensitivity and intensity.

Built on the backs and the strength of the people,
Despite fear and relentless aggression by defeaters.
Our strength and shield from offensive intruders,
Only forces our nation to become the aggressor.

Where are we now, and where will our strength come from,
That is needed to defeat the aggressors who hate us?
Why have they come to the country of the free,
If they resent the freedom, we possess and breathe.

We must continue to rebuild and gain strength,
To fight for our freedom and rights we possess.
We must build on our faith and rely on our God,
To help us protect and defend all we've got.

We must thank God for the good and ask to protect,
The hungry and weary that wish for the best,
We must take from our forefathers their strength to hold tight,
The freedom we now have and will hold through the night.

We've taken a few steps backward on the battlefield of freedom,
We've given into the greed so many pledges to behold.
We've stumbled and fallen into the arms of the greedy,
Without a thought for those who are needy.

Why have we followed instead of leading,
And taken the easy road we were given?
We must take a tact and one giant step back,
To preserve the hundreds of years we've been given.

Our freedom is threatened and our lives left pending,
The selfishness of others who are jealous of our freedom.
We must stand tall and bare our strength,
To preserve this land for the young and the living.

WHERE HAVE I BEEN?

Feel like I'm in a fog,
Or under a spell.
It feels like I've been gone,
For an awfully long while.

Have I been unconscious?
Or possibly dazed?
I feel years have passed,
Since you held me last.

What have I missed?
Besides you, my dear?
Has it been quiet,
Without me here?

What's that you say,
It has only been an hour?
I'm awakening from,
A bit of rest?

"My dear, it was only a dream,
I'm here with you now.
And I'll never leave,
Don't cry for me, I'm here."

MASKED FACES

Masked and hidden,
By thoughts of the past.
Remembrance of thoughts,
Of days long ago lost.

Days when we believed,
In miracles and hope.
Lost in the dismal darkness,
Thoughts of yesterday.

Severed memories,
Cut from the heart.
Left to die,
Lonely and adrift.

Lost are others,
Shattered dreams.
Life has forgotten,
To remember their dreams.

Masked are the prayers,
For a new tomorrow.
In the hopes of life,
That's been borrowed.

Lee Christine Brownlee

Liquid Smile

Liquid builds,
In the corners of my eyes.
Then blinds me,
With a flood of tears.

I sit and wonder,
When will they stop?
Obstructing my view,
Of the truth.

The smile is only a camouflage,
That hides the real pain I feel.
The sadness of a lifetime felt,
Won't wash away my tears.

I've mastered this smile,
That I wear each day.
I can take it off, or put it on.
It's the smile that suits my face.

TRAIN RIDE

As I catch a glimpse,
Of faces around me.
Attempt to decipher glances,
Reading lines in their faces.

Sallow appearances,
Weep to remember,
Broken promises,
That once caused the pain.

Eyes that once held a sparkle,
Are now hollow and empty.
Barely resemble,
Eyes that once smiled.

Dried and wrinkled lips,
Once kissed someone.
Hold less moisture,
Than a tiny drop of rain.

Life has shuffled the spirit,
Replaced the smiles with sadness,
But the lines in the faces,
Reveal their entire story.

PETALS

Rose petals,
Still moist to the touch.
Their withering fragrance,
Blends into the air like dust.

Petals falling,
Atop one another.
A mound of fragrant petals,
Potpourri in the rough.

Air blankets the moisture,
The petals begin to dry.
Dried petals after days,
Begin to smell like death.

Discolored and shriveled,
As death treats us all.
Rose petals are treated,
With remorse.

DREAM NOT

Dream, not those beautiful dreams,
For fear of awakening to a nightmare.
Dream not for fear of reality,
When you become the reality of your dreams.

Fear of life as seen in dreams,
Brings daunting memories of sadder times.
Thoughts of happiness are distant,
When dreams are invaded by reality.

Lack of devotion and fear of awakening,
Weakens the spirit and joy of living.
Stroll through your life-scape,
Behind the scenes of your dreams,
Revisit the reality, as it's perceived.

THE LONGEST WAIT

Writer, with pen in hand,
Awaits each thought,
To reach his fingertip.
Paper and pen await.

Wait is delayed,
Then, like a river's rush,
It flows…
Ripples off the tip of the pen.

Flows freely,
Spilling out thoughts,
In rhythmic style, ever flowing.
Like a river's mouth,
Overflowing with words,
Into a sea of emotion.

The flow suddenly ceases,
As if the river bed has dried up.
Leaving a dusty residue,
In its wake.

When will the tip
Of the pen refill?
With new thoughts,
Spilling out like sand,
In an hour glass.

Endlessly waiting,
The pen is motionless.
Thoughts fail to return.
Never to be replenished,
Pages have yellowed with age.

Sadness fills life,
Searching for the words,
Never to again appear.
A sea of emotion,
Withered and dry.

VIEW FROM THE INSIDE

The gentle softness in your eyes,
Devours my emotions.
Drapes me in comfort,
Consumes my soul,
While filling my heart with new sensations.

FINAL STEPS

She eased into her senior years,
Reaching out for the final good-bye.
Who is left to assist her,
Over the last threshold of life?

WHISPERING WIND

A window is open just a crack,
I hear a whisper — "I'm back."
Beckons me to open it wider,
So the sound could be much louder.

Step by step, the closer I get,
The sound becomes louder to my ears.
What sound is that I hear,
A voice, or whispering wind?

Can it be a sound so sweet,
A voice I've heard before?
Or a voice I wish to hear,
Again from someone not so near.

This sound that beckons me,
Friend or foe — I wonder?
Do I imagine this whisper?
Maybe it's only a spell I'm under.

Voices in the wind whispering to me,
"Come and help me in."
At long last I hear it loud and clear,
"I've been calling you for years."

As I stumble to the windowsill,
Not quite assured, but listening.
Who is whispering to me?
"But I have returned from far away."

The whispering wind begins to whistle,
Louder and louder as I move closer,
Why do you keep whispering to me?
Just open the door and come in and see.

DARE TO DREAM

Dare to dream big, and far,
Reaching for those dreams up high.
Grabbing the edge of time,
Wondering just how high you've climbed.

Take hold of the edge of your dream,
Stretch it as far as you can.
Filling in the open spaces,
With bright colors etched in love.

Dare to dream when no one thinks,
Those dreams could possibly be achieved.
Holding on tight to opportunities,
Building your dreams so they come true.

Top off your dream,
With happiness and love.
Always remember,
How far you've come.

You may have to take a few steps back,
Regroup your thoughts and plans.
Rebuild a couple of steps,
To reach the top rung to rest.

When you have reached your goal,
Turn around and help those struggling.
Share your strength, open your heart,
Helping others is what makes it worthwhile.

TEMPERED MOMENTS

Proclaiming injustice,
Only flares the tempers.
Of those enacting,
Hurtful scars on others.

My temper flares,
Like an exploding star.
The injustice enacted,
That leaves those scars.

Lee Christine Brownlee

DEATH OF A STAR

Stars that sparkle, lighting our path,
You wonder how long they'll last?
View of a shooting star,
Disappearing into the darkness,
Dims as it passes overhead,
On its last voyage in the sky.

Where do stars go when they die?
Is there a place for dying stars?
Have they used up all their energy,
Twinkling and lighting the skies?

Stars, die, lose their glow,
Fall from the sky,
While they disintegrate turning to ash,
Before our eyes.

Their ashes are spread over the skies,
That might serve as a cushion,
For other stars that fall when they die.

Who watches over the stars,
To ensure their twinkle is seen?
Charting their movement through the skies,
Noting the distance traveled thus far.

Sparkling and glowing for us to admire,
Bringing happiness to the skies as they sparkle.
Who will light our way when they die?
Is another star born to continue the brilliance,
When another star has lost its energy to shine?

See them sparkling from far away,
Wonder if they will be there tomorrow?
Twinkle… Twinkle… Twinkle… Twink… T…

LONELY PLANET

Loneliness eludes, no one.
Lonely for a friend,
To love, or be loved?
No escape to be found.

Stray animal at your doorstep,
Abandoned or lost.
Still suffers loneliness,
Longing to be loved.

Await the tender caress,
Of a human for love.
No matter how large the planet,
Or how small the village,
It is a lonely planet,
When you are searching for love.

It does not take a village,
To raise a child.
Only takes love and a smile.

CHASING SHADOWS

Each day I drift in thought,
Chasing a shadow through,
An abandoned street.

With each step, I am closer to the shadow,
I reach out, strain to touch,
But the shadow slips through my fingertips.

I run, and run, trying to catch up,
With the faded image before me.
Stumble, pick myself up,
And the shadow awaits.

Waits for me to again get close,
Just out of reach of my touch.
I can't grab hold of the faded image,
I can only feel the closeness,
Then it disappears.

I awaken, my face is moist and flushed,
Fearful of what might happen,
If I am able to grab the shadowy figure,
Will it disappear forever from my thoughts?

THE SHORT AND LONG OF LIFE

Life is too short,
When you are sharing,
Time with those you love.

Life is long,
When you are thinking,
Only of yourself.

SORRY I'M LATE

He'll never walk through that door again,
Calling out, "Sorry I'm late!
I got tied up talking to the guys,
And the time just slipped away.

You will forgive me, please?
You know how much I love you!
I get into trivia with the guys,
And we get carried away."

Then my thoughts stop racing,
From disastrous happenings,
To minor incidents.
He's home, he's safe, and I'm happy!
Another day to have him near me!

The years came, and the years went.
And my love returned each night.
Early, or late,
He returned safely to our home.

But one night I waited,
I prayed, and I waited.
Yet the front door never opened,
With his comforting callout,
"Sorry I'm late!"

The years have passed,
And time has healed the wounds.
Yet I still find myself waiting to hear,
"Sorry I'm late!
I got tied up again…
With the guys."

Recapture

Recapture faded and lost memories,
Rebuild a life once filled with joy.
Renew and reacquaint,
Duplicates sadness again reborn.

Lee Christine Brownlee

THEY STARE

The Man in the Moon stares each night,
With a quizzical look in his eye.
Checking to see if I'm happy or sad,
Or in need of a friend from the sky.

The Sun smiles each morning,
As I awaken and begin my day.
She also stares from above,
To see if I'm happy or sad.

The view from the galaxy,
Is filled with questions from the Stars.
What can they do to make me smile,
But twinkle and blink from afar?

ENOUGH TIME?

There is never enough time,
In a lifetime of dreaming.
To imagine how you would,
More wisely spend each hour.
Creating beauty for you to behold,
Caressing each rose petal,
As it's falling.

Changing each minute,
Into blissful existence.
Caring enough to fulfill,
All your dreams and wishes.
Creating new memories,
For you to treasure.

FRIENDS

Close friends are so few,
The numbers are small,
But the friendships that matter,
Are always there for you,
When you call.

BITTERSWEET

Sweetness of youth,
Justice for the innocent.
Bittersweet results,
Of adults and youths.

Lee Christine Brownlee

Reverberation
FIFTY-TWO FLUTTERS PER SECOND

A Hummingbird hovers,
Suspended in the air.
Reverberates the sound,
Of its wings that flutter.

IN LOVE

Never thought I could love,
Anyone as much as I love you.
Would not have shared my life,
With anyone else for sure.

Have felt so emotionally secure,
Since you came into my life.
My need for you is like,
The need to sleep and breathe.

To have you near me,
Is a dream I have wished.
Await each morning,
To share another day of bliss.

Lee Christine Brownlee

Forget Me Not

Baskets filled with blue Forget-Me-Nots,
Fragrance filling the air around us.
Surrounded by days more memorable,
When you forgot me not.

Today I go through the motions of life,
With far less enthusiasm.
Every day is less joyful,
Awaken each day less thrilled.
Still surrounded by Forget-Me-Nots.

I'M SO SORRY

I'm so sorry for the things I've done,
Sorry for the things I've said,
I don't know what came over me.
Please forgive me, I'm so sorry.

I thought you didn't love me anymore,
So I was childish and acted badly.
I didn't realize you were feeling the same,
I'm so sorry, I have hurt you this way.

Each night before I fall asleep,
I thank God I have you in my life.
I can't imagine a day without you,
I'm so sorry, for acting that way.

If you'll forgive me for my behavior,
I'll remember this night forever.
Never, never, treat you this way again,
Won't you forgive me, I'm so sorry.

CRYING CLOUDS

When the rain has stopped,
And the sun comes out,
Where do the brokenhearted,
Hide their tears?

No Longer Welcome

Moments of disbelief and sadness,
Failed promises of love forever.
Broken heartfelt with every crack,
Dreams washed away with tears.

Struggle to remember the beginning,
That feeling of ecstasy long gone.
Dreaming of a future together,
Never thinking it would fall apart.

What was the cause for concern,
The warning signs that went unnoticed?
Was it love or lust that carried us through,
To the tragic end we've became?

Who is to blame for the failed love?
Was it neglect or lies from the start?
Who led me on to break my heart,
Never again a harmonious beat be heard.

Did you know you would break my heart,
When you lied and told me you loved me?
Did you care how much you would hurt me,
With your unkind intentions from the start?

Do you think I will wait for your return,
Begging forgiveness for what you have done?
Open my arms and welcome you back,
So you can plot and plan your next attack?

Lee Christine Brownlee

Please walk away, don't look back,
Pick up speed as you depart.
You are no longer welcome near my heart,
You have worn your welcome out.

ENDLESS DREAMS

We visit in my dreams,
Watching you, watching me.
Thoughts are always centered,
Around the last days, we were together.

Dreams bring me peace and solitude,
Knowing I can revisit — no hesitation.
These dreams have kept you near me,
My thoughts inhabit these dreams.

Dreams I share with you are innocuous,
Innocent, yet monolithic in time.
Private dreams, yet broadcast,
To the heavens on high.

When will these dreams come to an end?
Hope never in my time here on earth.
When will they fade away — disappear?
Hope never, till I fade away with my dreams.

Lee Christine Brownlee

MEADOWS BLOOM

As I meander along the meadows edge,
Inhaling the beauty and fragrance that surrounds me.
The meadow glistens in the morning dew,
A field covered in wildflowers and clover.
Spellbound by the scent of the flowers,
And the beauty of the entire field in bloom.

In the distance, the sturdy woods begin to appear,
Broadcasts its shield that surrounds this secret meadow.
As breathtaking as this appears, the meadow houses,
The delicate fragrance caught by a breeze,
Enlightens my senses before it vanishes into thin air.

As I walk through the meadow,
Feeling the dampness of moisture under my feet.
Wandering freely touching petals and leaves,
With my fingertips, breathing in the scented air.
Looking back over my shoulder,
Glancing at my footprint path in the grass.

Drenched in the morning glow that adorns me,
Surrounded by the regalia of colors.
Transfixed on the woods surrounding this meadow,
I continue my journey to the trees in the darkness.
The sun has eluded the woods,
Darkness prevails, igniting a musty aroma,

The woods hold their secrets,
Dampness keeps the protective moss alive.
Plant life thriving on the open air,
Not diminished by the filtered sunlight,
Striking the trees from afar.
Lighting a path from sunlight to darkness.

Touch solitude and smell aloneness,
Swaddled in moss and ferns beneath my feet.
I rest, absorb the beauty, again looking back,
At the meadow lit by the sun and fed by dew.
Bewitched by the appearance of solitude,
Senses awakened to this hypnotic captivation.

Lee Christine Brownlee

WALKING ALONE

Walking life's path alone,
Wonder which way to turn.
Ignite a spark of life,
Beyond nightfall, where darkness looms.

Wish for someone to hold onto,
Share my thoughts and fears.
Hope as I round each corner,
The shadow will disappear.

Daylight befalls the saddened,
Nighttime welcomes me home.
Filled with hollow emotions,
Hope for a spark to ignite.

Walking alone through daylight,
Eases the sadness I feel.
Till a shadow appears to remind me,
I am shadowing my own fears.

Dream and wish for sunny days,
Hope for clouds to move on.
Want the life I long for,
To embrace and fill this void.

You in My Life

My life began the day I met you,
All my sadness began to disappear.
I knew I'd found my mate for life,
And happiness forever would be.

I can't look back in time in my past,
All those unhappy memories are fading.
A new beginning of a wonderful life,
Now that I have found you at last.

The precious times we spend,
Just sitting and doing nothing.
The mornings when I open my eyes,
I can't believe you are still in my life.

The happiness you have brought me,
Reveals nothing but bliss.
Creating all the wonderful memories,
We'll share throughout the years.

I can't imagine my life without you to share,
The wonderful times we have.
I count the hours we're apart,
Right down to the minute we reunite.

Thank you for being there,
Creating all new happy memories.
You in my dream, my heart's desire,
My life is now complete.

Lee Christine Brownlee

AFRAID TO LOVE

Afraid to give my heart away,
How many bumps and bruises can it take?
It's wearing thin for love again,
But will it recognize the heart to win?

He must be smart, with a big heart,
Loving and caring from the start.
I don't care if he has hair or is bald,
That doesn't really matter at all.

What's important is the gentle way he loves me,
And the way he holds me tight,
Just to let me know that every thing's all right.
That's what's important to me, you see.

It's not so necessary that he helps in the kitchen,
But it would be awfully nice if he did.
Mowing the lawn would be a treat,
But it's not the end of the earth to me.

The most important thing to me,
Is the wonderful person that he is,
The thoughtful and considerate man,
That would mean the most to me.

ALONE

Alone is one,
Can feel less than one.
Friends are many,
You're still alone.

Filling the hours alone,
Filling the hours with friends,
Still equals alone,
When one is alone.

The depth of alone,
Is measured by hours,
Hours tick by slowly,
When alone is one.

Friends stay in touch,
Their lives are filled with love,
Alone lacks love,
When alone is one.

Exhausted from sleep,
Filling the hours.
Sleep no more,
When alone is one.

Lee Christine Brownlee

Days are endless,
Nights are long,
Sleep eludes you,
When alone is one.

Alone with your best friend, yourself,
Equals two.

DREAMS ARE YOUR SECRETS

Dreams are nothing but secrets,
Of your wants and wishes.
Captured in your mind,
And saved for dreamy days.

Fond memories and wonderful thoughts,
Hold treasures and gems.
Of captured days gone by,
Or wishing well times.

We love to dream and pass the time,
Thinking of the happier events in life.
Recalling visions of the past,
Daydreams of wanton tomorrows.

Our daydreams can change,
Unhappy endings and the finale.
For a moment, you can script,
Your life and invent happier times.

Most of all when you see the finale,
It will be your version of the closing curtain.
Your recall of happier times,
You want to remember as a secret dream.

SCENE TO REMEMBER

See the harbor lights reflect the moon,
View the fishing boats tied to the dock.
I've waited for you to come home,
For as long as I can remember.

I'll continue to wait for your return,
For signs of you coming home.
I don't care how long it takes,
I'll be waiting for you to return.

The shadowy figure I see on the dock,
Resembles your silhouette from long ago.
Appears to be you returning home,
Tears moisten my cheeks once more.

Each day I prepare for your return,
Pour you a glass of wine.
Set a place at the dinner table and wait,
For your shadow to appear in the doorway.

It's getting late, I take a walk,
Down to the pier to see for myself.
Has your boat come in and docked,
And are you on your way home at last?

Stare at the harbor lights still reflects the moon,
Looking at all the people milling around.
Searching for your shadowy figure,
To glance my way and embrace.

Till the End of Time

My dreams have come true,
For my wishes professed.
I genuinely believe I've found my mate,
And will be yours for the rest of our days.

I waited so long for you to arrive,
Entering my life to complete this journey.
My search has ended and the reward received,
I'll be yours till time stops forever.

I am blessed by your jubilance for life,
And adorned by your lovely smile.
Shielded by your strength and desire,
Protected by the powers you possess.

Please let me know if my visions aren't real,
Or my presumptuousness premature.
Possibly I have been daydreaming,
For too long and realities askew.

If by chance I am not daydreaming,
Prick me with a pin to ensure I'm still alive.
The reality is genuine and true as defined,
I'll be yours till the end of time.

Lee Christine Brownlee

HALCYON DAYS

Halcyon days become more frequent with age,
As we wander down the road through life.
Days of reminiscence recalling times gone by,
Emerged in their reflection of life that once was.

Those lazy days spent staring at nature's beauty,
Thinking of childhood games played continuously all day.
Jumping rope, or teaching your dog a new trick,
Took all day while time appeared to be not moving at all.

Sitting on the sidewalk, watching the world pass us by,
Believing in miracles, ghosts and goblins that fly.
Passing time just tossing pebbles into a pond,
Or checking to see how deep the puddle really was.

Talking with friends, while planning your day.
Watching new construction buildings rise before your eyes.
Staring down sewers to see what's been lost,
And trying to save a bird fallen from its nest.

Sitting by the railroad tracks counting the cars,
As they chug along with cargo traveling far.
Then watching ants disappear and reappear,
In the cracks of the sidewalks by your feet.

Catching tree frogs and grasshoppers,
Just to watch them jump and play.
Wondering where they'll sleep at night,
Or hide when it gets too dark to play.

Sliding down grassy hills in cardboard boxes,
While enjoying the excitement of the unknown.
Lying in a hammock tied between trees,
Swinging back and forth just relaxing in the breeze.

Sitting in the park watching other kids play,
Hoping no one will notice you anyway.
Climbing and sitting high in the trees,
Watching the birds build and repair their nests.

Noting how spiders weave their webs,
While bugs explore what's happening there.
Life was so simple, yet complex at times,
The days filled with nothing but time.

ELUSIVE VISIONS

I view today as an elusive dream,
Reminds me of tomorrow's vision.
The dreams of tomorrow appear elusive today,
But are remnants of leftover scenes of yesterday's.

Subtle visions disappear when I blink,
Await return of yesterday's dream.
Will my elusive dreams elude my view,
Or escape without a moment's notice?

In the vast space, that surrounds our being,
What transparencies fill space?
Of wanton dreams and wishes,
That clutter our minds and aspirations.

Lasso those elusive visions and dreams,
And hang on tight to those remnants of scenes.
Don't waver or wander from those dreams,
There'll be plenty of tomorrows to spread your wings.

New Beginnings

Winter begins its final show,
And Spring begins its start.
From blossoms to falling leaves,
Sunshine to falling ice and snow.

The melting snow piles,
Swept to the side of the road.
The ground exhibiting growth,
Of blossoms to behold.

Trees sprouting their leaves,
And flower buds appearing to blossom.
New branches spreading their arms,
Welcoming each day's dawn.

Darkness appears later each day,
While Dawn is delayed each morning.
Earth continues to revolve,
And life continues to evolve.

Precious moments to behold,
Appearing without warning.
Life's beautiful memories,
Bursting with excitement.

The temperature has increased,
And the birds begin chirping.
They have hung out their nests to dry,
And returning to their family life.

Lee Christine Brownlee

The squirrels have come out of hiding,
Climbing and scrambling in the trees.
The old hoot owl is perched,
Out of our view and reach.

Spring is heading our way,
And nature is awakening to a rebirth.
The outdoors are alive and well,
Welcoming the joy of their fresh start.

EVEN THOUGH

How can the birds tweet the same tune?
How can life go on as if nothing happened?
How can I stop loving you,
Just because you're not around?

What makes life's simple pleasures feel great?
Where does time go when it flies by?
How can my life go on without you,
Just because you're not around?

Where is the one who finished my sentences,
And calculated my measurements in recipes?
How can I go on without you,
Just because you're not around?

No one to make my morning coffee anymore,
Or ensure I sleep in whenever possible?
Where's the one who hugged me,
Whenever it seemed, I needed love?

It was you who balanced my life,
Paved way for happiness to find me.
It was you who blessed every day,
With love, I needed to make my way.

The birds still tweet the same tunes.
Life goes on as if nothing happened.
I'm still, loving you,
Even though you're not around.

Lee Christine Brownlee

Child Within

Time passed, now we're older,
Pondering happy times enjoyed.
Thinking of childhood friends at play,
Wondering how friendships went astray.

Examining our lives so young,
Seems we had nothing but fun.
Recalling memories of today,
Finding such fault with life this way.

I question things so frequently,
Dislike the sadness and cries.
Resent unhappy times that clouded lives,
The paths we followed weren't always right.

Choosing paths that appeared so clear,
One that showed the road so sunny.
The paths we thought would lead our way,
To happy times with less dismay.

Where is that adventurous child,
With that sparkle in her eye?
The fearless child that lived inside,
Hidden so deep, and yet so wild.

Unsuspecting yet adventurous one,
The child is now a cognitive one.
Aware of dangerous paths,
That absorbs her life and cloud her smile.

Maturity has changed her life,
Stole the playful child, we liked.
Experiences that blurred her view,
The child within continues to play awhile.

CHOCOLATE BROWNIES

Hot baked homemade brownies,
Just out of the oven,
Is an invitation indeed,
To a chocolate feast.

Steaming aroma,
Spread throughout the house.
Brownies cooling on the windowsill,
Invites the chocoholic appetite.

Salivating while inhaling,
Await the temperature to drop,
Just enough to bite into,
My favorite chocolate stuff.

Toppings to indulge me?
Some dark chocolate chips tossed atop,
Oozing creamy swirls of decadent chocolate sauce,
Will certainly satisfy any chocolate thirst.

Laced with chunks of chocolate,
To lure any person.
Adding delight to the chocolate lover in me,
With shavings of pure milk chocolate indeed.

Melting and blending into a gooey morsel mess,
Salivating glands begin to ache,
Awaiting the first bite,
Of my chocoholic date.

CLEANSING TIDE

As you sit on the sandy shore,
Mesmerized by the rolling waves.
Rolling and slapping against the edge of the sand,
Slowly reaching your feet.

The tide withdraws to the ocean's depth,
Taking with it all your troubles.
While the sand soaks up the last layer of seawater,
Receding to its birthplace.

Little bubbles in the sand house escaping sand dabs,
Submerge themselves in the wet, sandy shore.
Again and again to return no more,
To replay their short life on the soaked shore.

Hypnotized by the rolling in, and rolling out,
The sand cleansed with each wave.
Slapping the shore, it recedes,
As do all of your sorrows.

Staring as each wave gets closer with every roll,
Soon the beach will be under water 'til tomorrow.
Your heart beats to the rhythm of the roll of the waves,
Never skipping a beat or rhythm of the ocean's roar.

This peaceful rhythm calmly tugs at your heart,
Each reassuring wave brings a soothing repose.
Of therapeutic rhythmic motion, soothing tenuous feelings,
Softening nerve endings to allow your escape.

Lee Christine Brownlee

Transporting you to a calmer place and time,
With every wave that returns.
Taking all your sorrows,
Cleansing them for a new tomorrow.

LIFE AND DEATH

Morbid curiosity,
Rubberneckers on the highway,
Expectations of disaster,
Agonizing cries of survivors.

Lost at sea,
Buried in water.
No flowers to keep,
Mourning cries of disaster.

Hurricanes and tornadoes,
Sweeping the land clear.
Leaving behind sadness, death,
And destruction for others to clean.

Burning buildings all ablaze,
The crackling of wood as it fades.
While flames grow taller,
Life appears to grow shorter.

The sadness of loss,
Pending tragedy.
The recovery from sadness,
Depends on our trust.

Lee Christine Brownlee

Rainbows in My Mind

Beauty in a dream,
Creates serenity in your mind.
Colors of your dream,
Spread beauty throughout time.

Richer the colors,
Growing more vivid in time.
Colors created,
Are rainbows in your mind.

Colors sharpen,
Becoming brighter, more dense.
The richness of these colors intensifies,
Rainbows' shades of time.

Stored in the corners of your mind,
Memories of passing time.
Secret places where dreams reside,
Rainbows glow and come alive.

Take a trip and visit this place,
Where dreams come alive,
And rainbows glow brightly.
Spend time with those colors in your mind.

Vulnerability

Erasing sad times,
Forget lost loves and defy.
Rid our conscious of sad endings,
And unfinished beginnings.

Afraid to give again,
Or love once more.
Keep from getting hurt,
Preparing for the worst.

Allow vulnerability,
Subject to failure.
Let our hearts forget.
Let our minds wander.

Rely on the future,
To heal past wounds.
Enabling our minds,
To make room for happier times.

Lee Christine Brownlee

FACES IN THE MIRROR

Who are the faces in the mirror,
Do they belong to me?
Have I something real to fear,
From those eyes staring back at me?

Seldom happy faces,
Stare into my eyes.
The visions in the mirror,
Clearly tell no lies.

Lonely eyes with deep concern,
Looking through their tears.
The tears of lost hopes,
That vanished through the years.

The sadness in their faces,
Reflect the fallen dreams.
Yet the visions in the mirror,
Appear to know it's me.

EPIPHANY

Wonder what will become of me,
After you're gone and life together has ended?
Who will comfort me when each day closes,
When I need your strength and understanding?

Wonder what will become of me,
When tomorrow delivers life's new problems?
Who will be there to hold me tight,
When I awaken each morning without your smile?

Wonder what will become of me,
When I grow older, and I'm alone?
Who will be there to comfort me,
And wipe my tears when I'm lonely?

Wonder what will become of me when I die?
Will you be there to comfort my cries?
Wonder what will become of me,
Without you after life.

I know what will become of me,
When the end is near.
You'll reappear and hold me tight,
While I cross over to the other side.

Lee Christine Brownlee

GATES OF HELL

Paralyzed by my own fears,
Yet my fears are merely cries,
Not dependent on my emotions,
Appearing without provoking.

Fears are dreams that won't come true,
Until my life has bled its tears.
Provocation of my fears,
Only paralyze those dreams.

What wounds of fear have opened,
Mask the lonely heart that's bled.
Paralyzed with fear of a new beginning,
Dare not expose the fear within me.

Distrust the many caring souls,
Claiming to want to help.
Fear of opening my soul,
Will let its tears within escape.

Darkness and distress,
My lonely heart won't open.
Locked up tight within its place,
The key is kept in darkness.

The key hidden from the Gates of Hell,
Won't open until the words are heard,
From my God and he has spoken:
Is this the place you dwell?

I slowly crawl out of Hell, stand tall at His feet,
Answer my God, no this is a place called Hell.
Await your hand to lead me,
To your place where angels dwell.

GOOD-BYE MY LOVE

Now that I have let you go,
I am lonelier than before.
The staircase to happiness,
Is never-ending and forever winding.

Now that I have let you go,
Can't cling to memories that once were,
Can't hold tight to the times that passed,
Must move on; create new times to have.

Now that I have let you go,
Can't hold tight to our lost love,
Can't hope for your return,
Must stop my heart from looking back.

Now that I have let you go,
You're free to mingle where angels dwell,
Free to wander; as I have cut the strings,
Released you from this world, I hold.

FALLING LEAVES CRY

In spring, the trees begin to renew,
The cycle begins to regenerate life anew.
Tree branches loaded with thousands of blossoms;
Blossoms exploding with beauty,
And filling the air with fragrance.

While gentle petals and nectar shine brightly,
Bees and butterflies floating in blissful obscurity,
Sipping nectar fortifying their life.
We too are drawn to fragrance filling our lungs,
And inflaming our senses.

The breathtaking exuberance of nature and its genius.
Renewal of spring rejoices in splendor,
Again, we know beauty has once more adorned us.
In fall the leaves slowly drift to earth,
Losing their moisture drying and cracking.

Slowly drifting to the ground,
As they drop from their branches.
While life evaporates from their leafy veins,
They harden and shrivel — I wonder if they feel pain?
Is it pain of sorrow that life is ending with no tomorrow?

Watching life drain from the leaves after falling,
Crackling sound under my feet while I'm walking,
Is that the sound of the leaves crying?
As the center of their existence,
Reminds us of the constant resilience of beauty.

Lee Christine Brownlee

Have the branches already started refreshing,
Or are they just resting?
Preparing for spring when new flowering buds appear,
Bringing life a new set of blossoms,
And begin the process into fall's final descent.

STROLL THROUGH SAN FRANCISCO

Jack London's home across the Bay,
Now crossing the Golden Gate.
Walking through Fisherman's Wharf,
Smelling the entrees as you pass restaurant doors.

While ships passing along the way,
Fishing boats pulling up to the dock.
Crabs are snapping at your heels,
Fishermen are unloading their catch-of-the-day.

Fresh sea air breeze from the shore,
Sunny days and foggy nights.
Smelling the kelp wash ashore,
Whispering sands upon the beach.

Watching seagulls wait and wait,
For crumbs on tourists' trails,
While the sun sets in the west,
Atop the ocean's crest.

Strolling through Chinatown,
Collecting your thoughts.
Sounds of shuffling feet,
With people busily working on a feast.

Buildings taller than Redwoods trees,
Towering over the City by the Bay,
The Financial District, quiet and clean,
Just remnants of a day's work seen.

Lee Christine Brownlee

The smell of coffee grinding,
Chocolate melting,
Sour Dough bread baking,
Your senses are on fire with taste buds aching.

Driving down the most crooked street,
Turning left; turning right,
Turning left; turning right,
Winding to the bottom of this twisted hill.

Up the hill,
Down the hill.
Turning right on a wrong way,
And down a one-way street.

Buses honking.
Delivery trucks double-parked,
People yelling,
"Get out of my way!"

The cable car bell clangs loudly,
While the conductor yells, "All Aboard!"
Passengers scrimmage grabbing for seats,
Before the cable car clangs through the streets.

The city's aglow like a Christmas tree,
Lights twinkling and street signals flashing.
There's so much you missed seeing while on this trip,
So plan another visit to this beautiful City by the Bay.

KALEIDOSCOPE OF DREAMS

The view from afar,
Delights and intrigues.
Every moment we sleep,
Weaves a kaleidoscope of dreams.

The colors changing.
Patterns rearranging.
Light entering the chambers,
Subdued in golden amber.

Dreams appear more vivid,
Striking and angled.
Constantly changing,
My kaleidoscope of dreams.

Awaken my senses,
Balancing my intentions.
Horizontally fixed and focused,
My kaleidoscope of colors.

The child in me explores,
The changing hues.
Sharp and crisp are the
Fringes of my dreams.

Time pauses...
The earth stops spinning...
The kaleidoscope is causing...
My dreams surrender.

Lee Christine Brownlee

Surrendering to a change,
Much brighter,
Much stronger,
More clearer than before.

The array of colors swiftly changing.
A bright new world of shades exploding.
Shades of colors never before presented,
In my kaleidoscope of dreams.

ARMY OF ANGELS

An army of angels,
Weave in and out of my life.
Filtering out only the sad and troublesome,
Allowing brilliant light inside.

Sunlight creates an aura around my angels,
That glows and surrounds me with love.
My army of angels creates an aura,
Around me and my life.

My army of angels continue,
To march while watching over.
Protecting me from dangers in life,
And the evils of others.

I hear my angels humming and humming,
While marching to the beat of my heart.
Their harmony is restful,
Protecting me all the while.

Dancing and singing in harmony,
They frolic in glorious splendor.
Bringing harmonious sounds,
That drape me in a robe of calm.

They bring me strength,
Weaving in and out of my dreams.
Never leaving my side,
As they keep me protected day and night.

Lee Christine Brownlee

FLIP-FLOPPING AROUND

The anguish of heartbreak,
The Amor of Love,
Wreak havoc on the heart,
While your subconscious flip-flops.

Over and over with every thought,
Twists and turns of a broken heart.
Relentless regrets and mindful upsets,
Present the heart with more flip-flops.

Protecting yourself and believing,
Calms your heart and relieves the stress,
To escape from your subconscious,
That causes your heart to flip-flop.

WEIGHT OF THE WORLD

The weight of the world on my shoulders,
The heaviness of the burden I hide,
Adds to the weight of my sorrow,
I'm carrying around inside.

Why me to pack this load?
Why not others bestowed?
Whose load is it I carry?
I carry the weight of the world.

Remember this heavy weight,
Set me free from sorrow.
Lift my shoulders high,
And balance the horror I hide.

Justice to all is required,
Balancing act inside,
Temper the anger around us,
Allowing peace to all who reside.

Lee Christine Brownlee

LAST LOAD

The load is heavy.
My heart surrenders.
The burden too much,
To carry alone.

Weighs me down.
Holds me back,
From moving forward,
To put down this heavy load.

My story is old,
No new lessons to learn.
Given much thought,
To this burden I carry.

My last load,
My heart can't take any more.
The heaviest cargo,
A heart can hold.

One last love,
To carry me through.
To the end of the road,
Love willing I hope.

Lost

Searching for beauty we lost…
Hidden remnants,
Of beauty misplaced,
In a world that has changed.

Lost beauty seldom found,
Reminds us of changing times.
Summer ends; fall begins,
Petals and leaves descend.

Gathered in piles all beauty ended,
Raked like fallen leaves and lost loves.
Nevermore to return,
No more life remains.

Holding remnants in our memory bank…
To retrieve at a moment's notice,
Bringing beauty we thought was lost,
Back to life — like the love that once was.

Lee Christine Brownlee

LOVE NEVER-ENDING

Rules and hearts should never be broken,
Torn apart or left unspoken.
Promises are forever and,
Love is never-ending.

Take not the heart and break it,
Or toss aside the rules that guide you.
Never forget the promises you've made,
Love will last forever.

Keep a mental list of those promises,
Tucked away for safekeeping...
As a reminder of those moments,
Never to be forgotten or broken.

Hold tight to the rules that guide you,
And new promises you make,
So not to harm or destroy,
Love never-ending.

LOST AND FOUND

I've loved and lost,
Then loved again,
Like blossoms in spring,
They die in the end.

Loves I've found,
Bring back to life,
Lost loves,
And forgotten times.

Sharing memories,
Of times in love,
Restores the feeling,
Of the emotional tug.

Lee Christine Brownlee

TEMPORARY INSANITY?

Is it temporary insanity,
Or only appears temporary?
Is it insanity,
Appearing to be temporary?

Is it controlled,
Manipulated and honed,
For special occasions,
And events only?

Temporary insanity,
Could merely be an excuse.
To temporarily misbehave,
Walking away free of guilt.

Do gray areas appear,
And make it temporary?
How short is the fuse,
From sane to insanity?

What were the clues,
Leading up to the cause?
Of insanity rolling over,
To temporarily insane?

MOVING

The stress of moving,
Packing memories for safe keeping,
Putting them in boxes,
Protecting them from losses.

What to keep?
What to toss?
Will I need it?
Will I not?

Sealing the boxes up tight,
To preserve their life,
Until a new home is found,
To bring them out in sight.

Unpacking those memories,
Pausing and dwelling,
Reliving their memories,
For an instant recall.

Lee Christine Brownlee

My Best

I am at my best,
When I am alone.
Because I allow myself,
To be my best.

I am the best,
When I am alone.
Because I like myself,
When I am at my best.

When I am with others,
I am at their best.
The best they want,
Me to be for them.

When I am with others,
I am at their best.
The best they will allow me to be,
But that's not me.

But Doctor!

I grabbed the bag,
That holds my heart,
And looked inside,
For all the parts.

What could be missing,
That acts as the glue?
Holds it all together,
And pumps it through?

It must be love,
That feeds it life,
And holds,
All the pieces tight.

What does it take,
To mend a broken heart,
And fill in the gaps,
Till it's all one part?

Will it take a lot of work,
And time to heal?
Or will it escape,
With just a bit of glue?

What makes it pump,
In such beautiful rhythm?
Does it come natural,
Or is it a symptom?

Lee Christine Brownlee

Can this be purchased,
Off a shelf like a toy,
Or is it something,
That warrants more?

Can you tell if your heart,
Is smart, happy, or sad?
Does it warn you of dangers ahead,
By speeding up and slowing down?

Has it spoken before,
And went unheard?
Or maybe it's afraid,
I never notice when it hurts.

In that bag of parts,
Are you sure they're all accounted for?
Or is anything missing,
Because I don't feel the mend happening?

Can a heart be too tired,
To make the glue harden?
Does it have one more mend,
In its bag to bargain?

Or have I used up all options,
To mend this broken heart?
Will my heart ever feel again,
That rhythm do blips?

Can the mend happen,
Without the love?
Or will it need new love,
To generate beauteous rhythm?

Lee Christine Brownlee

MY HEARTACHES

My heartaches,
For love,
Not just any love,
But true love.

The hole in my heart,
Has saved space,
To fill with love,
Of a long forgotten face.

It's been years,
Since I've been held,
By a significant other,
With love I've felt.

By someone special,
To mend the holes,
Of an empty place,
Once filled with gold.

Emotional closeness,
The feeling of love,
Will again be exploding,
From within and above.

As once again,
The hole slowly fills,
With that somatic feeling,
That only love knows.

That empty chamber,
Awaits this sensation,
That fills with affection,
And elation.

Halfheartedly filling,
Will it be filled,
With the enthusiasm,
It once knew?

How long will it take,
For that love to arrive,
To fill this gaping hole,
In my heart before it dies?

I've been waiting and waiting,
But dare not cry,
Will it fill,
This empty chamber inside?

I feel it getting closer and closer,
It is rushing in at top speed.
My long awaited love has arrived,
And never again to leave.

Wait!
Is this true, or just an illusion?
But my heart wouldn't deceive me,
Or mislead me, would it?

Oh no…
I believe I have only been dreaming.
Maybe another day,
A new beginning.

My Heart Is on the Mend

Oh my goodness, my heart is on the mend,
That old feeling is coming back again.
What is this mysterious fix?
Could it be my heart playing tricks?

I feel it thumping just as strong as before,
It has mended and is reopening its door.
Falling in love just as before.
Let's not play tricks on this old heart anymore.

Taking the plunge,
For the last time in this life.
Has my heart met someone wonderful,
Where it wants to reside?

Jump aboard that love boat, row ashore,
It's taking the plunge and giving a shove.
It's the happiest it's been,
In a long time in love.

Must be special,
To have brought new life to my heart.
If I'm dreaming, don't wake me,
My heart might fall apart.

Lee Christine Brownlee

THINGS I MISS

I miss the chats about nothing urgent.
I miss the conversations about what's important.
Most of all I miss the times,
Times we spent just sitting and talking.

We agreed and disagreed,
Now conversations are over.
The only one is me,
And I must play all the parts.

Shopping for food is difficult,
My habits don't realize I've bought too much.
The years of shopping and cooking for two,
Keep haunting me when I'm not cooking for you.

Movies we watched are now in the past,
Look for old reruns to recapture those laughs.
Music still plays and the concerts still heard,
But my heart still searches for that echo of laughs.

I'm getting better at accepting you're gone,
I'm hopeful that time will help me move on.
Looking for new love to revive those old feelings,
Can only be felt by the heart that is healing.

A FRIEND

To have someone to share everyday feelings,
From the exasperating commuters,
To the obnoxious shoppers,
Reposes daily stresses.

Trading wisdom and kindred spirit,
Escapes the feeling of loneliness,
And drops the moat to let someone enter,
Your secret place called home.

Germinating seeds and potting plants,
A constant gardener that never looks back.
Feeding and caring of nature's plantation,
Birthing life's beauty of garden creations.

Easier sharing inner feelings,
With someone you can trust.
Exchanging thoughts and opinions,
With someone you can call a friend.

(Poem written for a dear friend, K. E. Branch. Thank you!)

Lee Christine Brownlee

PINK ROSE

The break of day,
A breath of air…
Beauty is more,
Than eyes can bear.

Life renewed —
Each breath we take,
Brings new light,
To the beauty of day.

Each petal unfurls,
Yet revealing another.
Gift from nature —
Secretly hidden under.

What compares,
To nature's gift?
Reveals her secrets,
Each day that passes.

Moment by moment,
View of life.
Prevails no matter,
What the plight.

Taking each breath,
Repeating this beauty —
Like slow motion revealing,
Life's unfurling journey.

Capturing our hearts,
The petal unfurling,
Exposing beauty,
Only she beholds.

Like the rose,
Capture their hearts,
Expose your beauty within,
For the world to behold.

PLEASE

Please don't mourn me when I'm gone,
I laughed, I teased, I loved, I wept.
The many years I worked and lived,
The best were years we hugged and kissed.

The times we shared, the laughs we had,
Are memories that will last.
Important times are the times I held you tight,
And those will last throughout your life.

The bad times should be forgotten,
They are not worth another moment of time.
The sad times, hopefully are gone,
But the good times will linger on.

My time is up and I must move on,
I'm only making space for another person to rest,
My journey has ended and I'm traveling on,
Please don't mourn me when I'm gone.

QUICKSAND

Is it love, or is it quicksand?
You feel the tug on your heart.
The millions of grains of sand,
So quickly pull you under.

Displaced among the grains,
Your heart makes room for another.
Can you fight the strength,
Of the force that's pulling you under?

Do you give in or continue to struggle,
Relax and let it consume you?
Quicksand is swiftly moving faster,
As you give in to the love that follows.

The shifting of sand so gentle yet swift,
It captures your body, and soul in its grip.
The more you fight, the quicker you sink,
The harder it tugs at your heart to give in.

Love is like quicksand,
Step softly and gently.
Ensure the ground beneath,
Is firm with both your feet on the ground.

Your heart is captured,
You have succumbed to its force.
Love is like quicksand,
Just give in and enjoy.

Lee Christine Brownlee

REGRETS

We all have regrets,
Some people have many.
The should'ves,
And could'ves are plenty.

Learn from regrets,
And build new tomorrows.
Allowing others to enter,
Your new array of color.

Change your hue,
Add bright thoughts and views.
Moments in your rainbow,
Add colorful memories of the new you.

Sacrifice and Die

We leave behind the trampled souls,
Leave the land to bury its own.
Our prayers go out to all who gave,
Their lives so precious to those they saved.

So much unrest today.
Was there always so much hate?
Is it the population growth?
That makes it appear much more unrest?

Is it unrest that makes it appear?
To show such detest of life to fear?
I catch a glimpse of those who died,
So I may live a safer life.

Worn uniforms show wounds and wear,
Their life was drained so mine was spared.
How can we repay those who died?
When we selfishly fail to live with pride.

Repaying those sacrificed lives,
Stand up what is right!
Give respect and thanks,
For the soldiers who died.

Lee Christine Brownlee

Solace

Bringing solace to my heart,
Softens the crusty edges.
Of heartbreak and sorrow,
Offering peace to enter my soul.

Stillness of breath,
Sadness of passing time,
Alone inside my aching heart,
Echo's the heartbreak of silence.

Kiss of morning light on my eyes,
The sound of birds chirping in the trees.
Lends solace to my mind,
While the earth releases a quiet breeze.

Tiny waves rolling on the sandy shore,
Caressing my soul with each slap of a wave,
While it recedes and erases the scars,
Etched on my heart and soul.

My body overcome with calm,
Accepting no pain or sorrow.
The sandy shores of my heart refreshed,
Renewed with harmony and repose.

Arriving at the end of the journey,
Welcoming a new beginning.
Eternal peace and well-being,
Solace takes over as my heart is healing.

STUMBLE AND FALL

Stumble and fall,
Pick up, start over.
Life's a continuous treadmill,
Beginning to end.

The race is on,
Who is in front?
If he stumbles and falls,
Will he begin again?

Life has started.
Stumble and fall,
No bones were broken,
After all.

The terrain gets steeper,
The speed increases.
Are you gaining or losing,
This race in life?

Fall to the wayside,
Stumble and fall.
Life's dangerous path,
Belongs to us all.

Lee Christine Brownlee

MY STUPID, STUPID HEART

My heart is educated,
But not too smart.
Sometimes it doesn't —
Listen when I talk.

We have these daily meetings,
With graphic demonstrations.
On what a smart heart,
Should never embark.

But my stupid, stupid heart,
Thinks it knows all.
It falls in love,
And thinks it's smart.

One day it will awaken,
And wish it had listened,
To the voice it never hears, saying,
"Not again, my stupid, stupid heart."

TAKE A CHANCE

Like to take a chance on love.
Wonder if the odds are like the lottery?
Do you think it comes in scratch-off form?
Or maybe there will be a loud drum roll warning.

How can I tell if I've missed the call?
Does it come with a very loud bell?
Maybe it has all the bells and whistles,
So I won't have to listen for the call.

Is there someone who could take a message,
Just in case I'm in a meeting?
But how many rings do you think I'll hear,
And is the bell loud and clear?

Maybe I'd better sit here and wait,
Just in case that call comes in.
But who's to say it will be a call?
Maybe I'll hear a knock on the door.

I'll sit patiently and wait for the ring of the bell,
Or the knock on the door.
I have time, don't I?
Oh, what the hell,
I've got lots of time to wait.

Lee Christine Brownlee

Spinning like a Top

My head is spinning like a top out of control,
Thoughts seem to be taking their toll.
The spinning is wobbling it to and fro;
Don't know how to get things back under control.

If I spray some stabilizer into the air,
This might slow the wobbly motion I fear.
Maybe if I sit still, monitor my thoughts,
Get control so I can manipulate the source.

Baggage I carry in my head weighs me down,
I have too many things I worry about.
My burdens are an encumbrance to my logic,
I need to bring the spinning thoughts to a halt.

How simple it would be if we could implement a switch,
That would regulate the load of the baggage we tote.
The switch could be placed at the height of our waist,
We could manipulate the load thus controlling our fate.

Spinning, spinning, spinning like a top,
My thoughts whirl around like sand in the wind.
My imagination excels to high speeds as it swirls,
On the edge of my conscious thoughts of those spinning cells.

Wading through sleepless nights,
And adding up the uneventful flights,
Keeps me hopelessly in doubt,
That I will be able to control my plight.

My head is spinning like a top out of control
Life seems to be taking its toll,
And the spinning is wobbling to and fro...
I am no longer in control.

Lee Christine Brownlee

THOSE WERE THE DAYS

I had a wonderful phone conversation,
With my cousin Ray.
We laughed like we were kids again,
And we talked about the days back then.

We remembered all the fun things in life,
The aunts, uncles, and others we liked.
We lived in the best of times,
And cried through the saddest times.

Respected our parents,
And their decisions,
Although we often disagreed,
With some of their reasoning.

Believed in love forever,
And family dinners were to be remembered;
But our love for our country, jazz, and God,
Would never waiver, our family life was always favored.

Today is different,
Respect is gone,
But we hang tight to our past,
In the hopes of it coming back.

We remember our youth,
And remind each other,
Of those days gone by,
In the hopes of another try.

Times were simpler,
Less stressful, less fearful,
But it was important to remember,
Dinner was at seven.

We had our chores and responsibilities,
And we did them all without too much gawp.
If we didn't, we'd hear about it at dinner,
And the results were inevitable without a squawk.

The bantering between siblings,
Was intense at times,
But no one else,
Was allowed to criticize.

It is terribly sad in today's busy world,
That no one sits down to dinner with the folks.
Everyone's personal world is too busy to communicate,
That lost art so often left to disintegrate.

How can they hold on tight to each other,
If all they offer is a glimpse of one another.
We contact our grown children as often as we can,
Without invading their personal plans.

If we don't contact them weekly,
They start questioning our mentality,
And start thinking we're out of touch,
With reality.

We try to be aloof,
When it comes to our activities,

As grown children,
Can't believe our agility.

As years pass by we can only hope,
We've left our mark to help others,
In remembering the importance,
Of family first.

(Taken from a phone conversation with my cousin, Raymond Torres on
October 17, 2013.)

Taking a Ride on My Memory-Go-Round

Took a ride on my memory-go-round.
A ride I take to survive, faster and faster,
Up and down, going round and round,
Creating a breeze and feeling free.

The scenery changes in my mind,
My favorite music in the background.
Up and down on my painted horse,
Replaying happy days on my memory-go-round.

Never-ending ride of a life.
The scenery changes, pictures rearrange,
Rolling hills and dreamy pastures,
Beautiful scenes spinning past me.

Mirrors magnify every dream,
Racing through time, grabbing at the ring.
Whirling and spinning back to the beginning,
Round and round the dream never-ending.

Memories appearing, symbols clanging,
Joyously recalling the ride of my life.
The memories returning, laughter sounding,
On this glorious ride on my memory-go-round.

Lee Christine Brownlee

WHISPERS AND SNICKERS

Whispers and snickers,
Bullies in the park,
Making life miserable,
For everyone sought.

Picking and probing,
Bullies in the park,
Making someone's life,
More lonesome than not.

Teasing and shoving,
Bullies in the park,
Picking on the kids,
Who everyone forgot.

Teaching a lesson to,
Bullies in the park,
Standing up to those,
Unlikeable sorts.

Make your mark,
Take part,
To stop those unwanted,
Bullies in the park.

MOONBEAMS AND SHOOTING STARS

Skyrocket sparks are flying,
My mind traveling so fast.
While flying through the heavens,
What on earth could be happening?

Moonbeams shooting,
'Round in my head.
Bouncing off stars,
As we round Mars.

The Milky Way trails,
While new stars appearing.
Lighting our way,
Past the comet display.

Starbursts of brilliant colors,
Announce their beauty with sparkle.
Instant life bursting in the heavens,
Revealing new life viewing earth tomorrow.

Dazzle and sparkle,
Blinking and winking.
Looking down on earth,
Enjoying its glitter.

Shooting stars pointing,
From the heavens to earth.
Glorious lights announcing,
Each new day's birth.

Lee Christine Brownlee

SHIPWRECKED HEARTS

Broken hearts resemble a shipwreck at sea.
The pieces crumble, some float to the surface.
Other pieces sink, never to be seen again,
But always remembered, never enjoyed.

Heartbreak resembles the tearing of memories,
Shredded lives and experiences.
Unforgettable moments of love,
Forever lost in the rubble of the wreck.

The havoc, the lost souls,
Having lived through the stormy debris,
Find a raft floating, a lifesaver of strength,
A shred to hang onto that beckons life.

New life to breathe happiness into every soul,
Reaches out to help and strengthen.
A branch of truth and happiness,
Soothes the wrecked endangered heart.

A cello plays on, the memories,
Of life as the wreckage is tossed about.
Pieces of lives ripped apart,
But long remembering the love.

A bow pulled across the strings of a cello,
Mesmerize the watchers and wonderers.
What will happen now, who will be saved?
What will become of the shipwrecked hearts?

The hearts stranded in a stormy sea,
Awaiting rescue from the dangers ahead.
Awakening to a quiet, calm day.
A day of repair and renewal on the stormy sea of love.

Lee Christine Brownlee

MUTED SHADES OF GRAY

I awoke and found,
My dreams fading away.
Turned to drab shades of gray,
Colors becoming translucent, muted.

Dreams that held happiness,
Unlocked worlds of joy.
Viewing the future through child's eyes,
Disappearing to faded shades of gray.

A child's interpretation of dreams,
Never doubting, full of wishful things.
Always spreading joy and happiness,
Laughter surrounds innocence.

The childlike naïve appearance.
Complexity of dreams.
Rapidly flashing and changing,
Building a carefree existence.

Life has faded that childlike dream,
Grow paler and less visible.
Almost colorless, translucent,
Await the rainbow of vibrant colors to return.

LIFE'S PATH

The path of life is long and winding,
Roads are filled with twists and turns.
The corners seem like hairpin curves,
Road bumps protect us from speeding.

Cautiously maneuvering in danger zones,
Taking our time to read all the signs.
Remembering the penalties for failure,
Will detour us from enjoying life's pleasures.

The object is to prepare for trouble,
Ahead on life's bumpy road.
When we neglect to pay attention to warnings,
We are surprised with the dangers around each corner.

Lee Christine Brownlee

MEMORIES FOR ALL TIMES

Memories carried through life,
Are kept safely in our minds.
The little section of our brain,
Called, Memories for All Times.

Memories tucked safely away,
Full of wonderful times we've had.
Categorized and alphabetized,
So we can recall them — at any time.
The sensor on this Memory Bank,
When alerted has instant recall.
The miniature librarian kept on-hand,
Is waiting for your call.

The moment the alarm sounds,
That a special memory is needed,
The emotional team jumps on board,
In search of the memory for this deed.

The team starts running around,
Causing a headache indeed,
While clambering about like a scout,
Searching for the key, no doubt.

The team inquires, is she happy or sad,
Mad or contrite, is she flipping off walls,
Or only stomping the floors.
I think I got it — she's lost her love.

Should we send in the clowns,
Or recall some happier times.
Let's send in wonderful memories,
Of happier days in time.

She'll be back to herself again,
Making new happy memories,
To lock up tight in that memory bank,
Called, Memories For All Times.

PLEASE RECONSIDER, DON'T LEAVE

We've quarreled many times before,
And said that we were through.
We can work these problems out together,
Please reconsider, don't say it's over.

My heart is broken,
And my life with you ended.
I regret my cruel words spoken.
Oh why did you listen to me now?

We've hurt each other so many times before,
But we've never parted ways.
We've always worked things out,
And stayed together somehow.

I beg your return,
Things will be different this time.
I miss you already,
Why did you listen to me now?

The hurtful things we say,
We never really mean.
We are only shouting in anger,
Please reconsider, don't leave.

WHISPERS

Hear the whispers of Autumn,
Sing farewell to Summer.
With a hint of Winter,
Earth balances its load.

The trees will be bare,
As leaves gently drift to earth.
Whisper in their sorrow,
Another year, another tomorrow.

Replenish the soil,
The sun regenerating for Spring.
Recaptures beauty to embrace,
The freshness life brings.

The beauty of Fall declares,
The end of this year's growth.
The rejuvenation and birth,
Of a new beauty to behold.

Nature's time to hibernate,
Regenerate and prepare.
To flourish in Spring,
To begin again next year.

Lee Christine Brownlee

MY ELUSIVE BRANCH

Guided through life by an elusive branch,
Found on every tree I pass.
This branch is special to my heart,
It watches over me… It's smart.

Protecting me from bumps and bruises,
My elusive branch is always in front.
It bears no fruit, or leaves,
It is just there being elusive, you see.

I hear giggling coming from its bark.
It's a funny branch with a good heart.
Stormy weather doesn't affect this branch,
It's on a mission, from the start.

It will appear in a tree out of nowhere,
And just pops out to let me know it's there.
This elusive branch is not my imagination,
Just look to the trees, and you'll see.

(Written for a dear friend, My Elusive Branch.)

Owl in the Tree

The owl, so sturdy, so brave,
Staring down from his perch,
High in the tallest tree.

Why his interest in me?
Recognizes a familiar face?
Who will be his next prey?

Is this the same owl from last week,
Who perched high in the trees,
Watching my every move?

Does he live there above us all,
Spending his time just watching?
Do you think he really gives a *Hoot*?

Lee Christine Brownlee

WALTZING THROUGH THE MILKY WAY

Waltzing through the Milky Way,
My partner leading the way.
The Minute Waltz is playing,
As we celebrate our day.

Holding me close to his heart,
We glide from star to star.
Turning and swirling around,
Scattering stardust upon our ballroom floor.

Using the stars as stepping stones,
Balancing on our toes,
While twirling and swaying,
On the spiral arm that glows.

The waltz is a magical dance,
Done lightly on your feet;
One… two… turn and swirl,
Till the stars begin to whirl.

Gliding across the galaxy,
Twirling faster and faster,
Lighting up the sky,
While on the edge of cosmic matter.

My dress is swirling as we spin,
Our shoes lit up like stars,
We dance so beautifully together,
All lit up like Mars.

The Minute Waltz playing faster and faster.
The tempo controlling our speed,
As we glide through the galaxy ballroom,
Of stars beneath our feet.

You Kept It All

There is nothing I can do,
Never thought it would happen to me.
I gave you everything I had,
You've left me so sad.

What will happen to me now,
I have nothing left to give.
What will tomorrow bring,
But more sadness and tears?

I haven't any love leftover,
Could you please return just a little.
I need that love to share with someone new,
You took everything I had given to you.

You don't need all the love I gave,
Just a little unused love will do.
Just enough to grow the love,
To give away to someone new.

Please return some of that love,
So I can find me someone new.
Someone who will love me,
As much as I loved you.

INTENTIONS

Awful intentions commonly,
Disguised as artful flirtations.
Toy with emotional destruction,
Leading to the disarmament of the heart.

The heart, guilty of nothing,
Struggles to maintain its beat.
Reluctant to surrender,
To the artful flirtations.

Unwanted flirtations,
Lead to the withdrawal of intentions.
Imbalance the intentions,
Of artful flirtations.

Lee Christine Brownlee

Roll the Film

My memory bank has prepared a viewing,
And the film will be continuously running.
A review of my life from start to finish,
With all the sad scenes cut and deleted.

This special showing will automatically repeat,
So if you've arrived late, don't worry.
My life story has been looped for your enjoyment,
The names have been changed to protect the viewer.

Joyous time and tears of happiness,
Have been set to Chopin and Mendelssohn's music.
Nocturne for piano,
Filled with delightful rhythmic pleasure.

Please be seated, sit back and relax.
Above all, No Smoking, please.
The snack bar will be closed,
During this showing.

If you contributed to the happiness of this life,
Please hold your applause till the film has ended.
Sit back and enjoy the film,
All profits will be given to the elderly.

Thank you!

A PENNY FOR MY THOUGHTS

If I had a penny for every thought of you,
I'd be the richest person in the world.
Streets would be covered with pennies,
And the skies would be bright and shiny.

I begin each day with the thoughts of your love,
Your smile just brightens my life.
A penny for my thoughts could fill an ocean,
If I had a penny for every time I thought of you.

The weight of the clouds would burst open the skies,
Sprinkling pennies everywhere to be found.
My dreams would be filled with love for you,
If I had a penny for every thought of you.

I can't sleep at night just thinking of you,
I lay in my bed just counting my pennies.
Then another thought of you…
And I have to start counting all over again.

One million and seven, one million and eight… oops.
Another thought of you…
One million and seven, one million… oops.
Oh the hell with it!

One, two, three, four, five, six, seven, eight…

Lee Christine Brownlee

MY EMOTIONAL HARP

You have reached into my heart,
And plucked the strings of my emotional harp.
My heart may need fine tuning,
Although it has a strong beat.

While swaying to the rhythm of my heartbeat,
It has a strong beat that can be heard from afar.
Strong or weak, maintaining that beat,
While searching for a fine tuned mate.

The beat of my heart works beautifully,
And the rhythm should not be disturbed.
While searching for a heartmate,
That will be faithful and maintain a steady beat?

My heart wants to mate forever,
Not 'til a new heart appears?
Don't strum the strings of my emotional harp,
Unless you intend to stay in rhythm forever.

DISPOSABLE HEARTS?

Some people treat hearts,
Like disposable parts.
Abuse, toss aside,
Mistreat and break.

Some don't give the heart,
The tender love and care it deserves.
Instead, they leave the broken heart,
To repair itself for a new start.

Hearts are not to be tossed,
In the trash at the end of the day.
Or mistreated as if,
They can be repaired and replaced.

Hearts are the glue,
That hold us together.
Give us strength,
And makes us feel better.

It takes a lot of care,
To repair a broken heart,
When someone breaks it,
And tosses it out.

It takes strength and resilience,
To mend, revive and bring back to life.
So, please be careful,
Before you break someone's heart.
It has no disposable parts!

No Flowers, Please

Send me no flowers,
Cry me no tears,
Just send me your love,
To last the years.

Love everlasting,
Remembering and embracing,
Love speaks all languages
Love has no limitations.

Send me no flowers,
They will only die,
Send me your everlasting love,
Love forever be mine.

Time has no boundaries
Life is too short,
Our stay on this earth,
Depends on our ability to hold on.

Relentless Love

The animals we love, are often abused,
Tortured and left to suffer.
The same animals, without hesitation,
Save lives, and protect us from others.

These same animals that would indubitably,
Sacrifice themselves and their lives,
Relentlessly protect our lives from harm,
Keep us warm and love us dearly.

And what do they ask in return,
For that relentless love, sacrifice,
And undying companionship?
Not much...Just LOVE.

They want to cuddle with us,
Keep us warm and protect us from harm.
Maybe sneak a snack from the plate
When we're ignoring, or out of sight.

Go for a walk, or sit and listen to us talk.
Nap on our clothes, so our scent is close.
This helps them to sleep more peacefully,
When we're not near.

They learn tricks, because it makes us happy.
They'd rather sit and stare at us with love.
Ears perk up when they hear us coming.
Yet these fur balls can't help but love us only.

They patiently wait for us to finish eating,
Hoping we drop something on the floor.
And when they hear the house keys jingle,
They beg to accompany us without thinking.

How can people abuse animals that love them,
Beg to be near us, and cry when we're away.
Love to be petted, pampered and spoiled,
And would give their life just to be loved by us.

Lee Christine Brownlee

SPECKLES IN FLIGHT

Morning light beaming through the window,
Dust particles floating freely in the light.
Thoughts and dreams somersaulting in the air,
Tiny speckles settling on the surface below.

The light details your thoughts,
Arranges your view of the particles,
Floating and swirling in the streaming light before you,
To be wiped away like the morning dew.

Though your thoughts are still developing,
Speckles are still settling.
You begin sorting your thoughts.
Begin arranging birth of new beginnings.

Speckles sparkling and swirling in flight,
Through the filtered stream of daylight.
Create awareness, yet subtle and endless,
Freedom of thought, speckles of life.

Never ending, never settling,
Fallout in the stream of light.
Speckles free falling in the air,
Constant streaming of speckles in flight.

SURRENDERED

Surrendered my heart,
And my dreams.
Gave my love to someone,
Who surrendered nothing.

But took my love,
Broke my heart,
Trampled my dreams,
That person I loved.

My emotions and dreams,
Shattered and crumbled,
Then tossed away,
Like rainwater down a drain.

Survival of the fittest,
To again embrace life,
By picking up the pieces,
Of my broken heart.

Hiding the scars,
Of my heart on the mend,
Dive back in the pool,
And start swimming again.

Lee Christine Brownlee

Move On

Since you have been gone,
It has been hard to move on.
I've tried and tried,
But I can't erase the memories of our past.

I sit and think of the wonderful times,
All the days and nights
We just sat and talked,
Or did nothing at all.

I'm still sitting and talking,
But alone as I recall.
No one to fill that chair,
Next to mine just passing time.

I'm still trying to move on,
But I don't have the energy.
Replacing you in my life,
Is the hardest thing I have ever done.

A new day has arrived,
Maybe I'll go outside for a while.
Meet some new people,
Hear a voice that's not mine.

Smell the fresh air,
Touch a breeze with my fingertips.
Listen to nature whisper in my ear,
"It's time to move on."

Wake the birds,
Alert nature, I'm moving on.
Moving on without you,
Where loneliness doesn't live.

Make new friends,
And begin life again.
Keep all my memories of you,
Locked up tight in my heart.

I Give You My Heart, But. . .

Don't hurt the heart that loves you,
It would give anything for your happiness.
Treat it gently, and handle it with care.
Above all, return the love you get.

Please be kind to this old heart,
The one that loves so you very much.
Handle this heart like you would your own,
It's been hurt before and left alone.

Remember, it will be hard to replace a heart,
That loves you as much as it does.
So please handle it like you do your own,
With lots of love and care from your heart.

If you honor these small requests,
You will never feel heartache.
This heart will love and care for you,
Till the day it beats no more.

THE FLAME WENT OUT

I'd melt when you held me in your arms,
I felt sheltered from all harm.
Nothing could hurt me, or penetrate,
Warmth and feeling when you held me.

When you entered a room,
I could feel the atmosphere change.
Never felt so vulnerable,
Willing to fall in love before.

The chemistry started to flow,
The air became thick.
The sense of loneliness disappeared,
When you walked across a floor.

I have never felt that sensation before,
Or lived those moments again.
What happened to all that charm?
Where has that flame gone?

Please bring back the arms,
That once held me so close.
Reignite the flame,
That once ignited my heart.

Lee Christine Brownlee

OUR NEVER-ENDING WALTZ

One, two, three twirl,
One, two, three twirl.
Cover the whole dance floor,
Over and over again.

Our dance of a lifetime,
You hold me in your arms,
While we perform,
Our never-ending waltz.

One, two, three twirl…
One, two, three twirl…
Twirl and glide,
Over and over again.

And again…

WHO CARES FOR THE ELDERLY

The elderly are placed in homes for care,
But is it the care they need for survival?
Maybe they need love and attention,
Shared by family who are caring?

The elderly people of today,
Were once the family who cared for us.
Why are they sent to homes to be cared for by strangers?
When we are the ones who should care for them.

Is it not our job to care for family at home?
Rather than send them off to another home?
Shouldn't we take care of our own?
Take care of the ones who cared and loved us?

It is difficult to care for the elderly,
But wasn't it just as difficult to care for us.
Didn't they sacrifice for us?
Isn't it their turn to receive our love?

Lee Christine Brownlee

A New Perception

The moon slips behind the mountaintop,
Sun reaches for the sky.
I linger just a moment,
Thinking you'll walk back into my life.

The days pass so slowly,
The nights seem to stand still.
Waiting feels endless,
As the minutes slowly pass.

The sky appears a fainter blue,
The rain falls in bigger drops.
The air does not smell as fresh,
My life seems to be stuck on pause.

My view of you as it appears,
I'm overwhelmed with joy.
Then realize my mind is playing tricks,
I have perceived this view of you.

Time allows my imagination,
To conjure secret dreams and wishes.
Distorts my perception,
That plays tricks on my vision.

BLOWING FREE

Balancing on the edge of the world,
Holding onto the air I breathe.
Running on my tiptoes,
Chasing the blowing breeze.

Hanging on tight to the air,
So I don't slip and fall through the cracks.
Hanging on as tight as I can,
Balancing on a point in time.

What if I stumble and fall?
Am I strong enough to hold on?
What if I can't get back up?
Will I slip through the cracks like dust?

Balancing on the edge of the world,
Meandering 'round and 'round.
Holding onto the air I breathe,
While balancing on that point in time.

The air is so thin — it's almost not there,
A view of the world looking at me.
Holding on tight to the air I breathe,
Chasing the wind blowing free.

Lee Christine Brownlee

SMILING EYES

At the end of each day,
You stare out the window and wait,
For daddy to arrive,
With his smiling eyes.

His truck pulls up in front of the house,
He walks slowly and enters.
His demeanor expresses exhaustion,
That renders sorrow and fear.

His tired eyes were bright that morning,
Now express tiredness from the day's events.
You rush to greet him and to your surprise,
His eyes are sparkling like Christmas lights.

Now the years have passed,
Daddy is now old,
Alzheimer's has taken control.
He doesn't remember much anymore.

He appears lost sitting on the porch,
Then all of a sudden he sees me approach.
Again has those smiling eyes and says,
Oh it's you honey, just seeing your face, now I'm okay.

The tears roll down my face,
Just to see those smiling eyes,
Once again happy and joyous,
To have me near him for a while.

(Written in memory of my Dad, who had Alzheimer's Disease. The best
years of my life were when he lived with me and we took care of him.)

THE REST OF MY LIFE

What to do with the rest of my life without you?
How should I spend my days and nights?
The hole that's left needs you to fill the hours,
Till my heart feels happiness and delight.

I sit and watch the sunrise each morning,
But there's no one sitting next to me.
I make two cups of coffee each morning,
But they end up being both for me.

What am I to do with the rest of my life,
Without you in it to share the nights.
The crossword puzzles go half finished,
While I wonder what I'll fix for dinner.

The years go by and the clock ticks on,
I'm still waiting for you to come home.
What will I do for the rest of my life,
Without you in it as the love of my life?

Magnificent Imagination

Add mystery to your life,
And beauty to your eyes.
Delve into the unexpected,
Sweet essence of the unknown.

A moment in time expands,
To endless passing of time.
Where each moment is filled,
With unplanned, ceaseless emotion.

A look, a glance from a stranger,
Brings excitement and desire.
As if the solar system has rearranged,
Its cosmic show for your pleasure.

Lighting the galaxy,
With stars that shine brightly.
Exhibiting an array,
Of excitement for your eyes only.

A view into the future,
Reveals life of mystery and intrigue.
Where all beauty of love,
Is delicately unveiled before your eyes.

Reliving this moment over and over,
Enjoying its beauty to perfect your day.
Embracing the thrill of excitement,
To be shared with whomever you choose.

Lee Christine Brownlee

Let your imagination expand to include,
Momentous heartfelt love and desire.
This to be returned by someone special,
Longing for the same emotional thrill.

MY HEART IS HEALED!

My heart is healed,
I'm ready for love.
Embracing the world,
Renewing myself.

My heart is ready,
Looking for my last love,
To share my world,
To join my rebirth.

My heart is healed,
Ready to take a chance.
Spread my wings,
Enjoy that feeling again.

Join the heart within me.
Feel the love between us.
Share the world inside,
A place called life.

Lee Christine Brownlee

WHEN SHE APPEARS

When she appears,
It is my silent call she hears.
She is not a vision or an apparition,
I'm startled, spellbound, and mesmerized.

It's a feeling of heaven sent,
With an overwhelming feeling of love.
When I feel her presence,
She has calmly arrived, and is by my side.

The emotional pain begins to ease,
My attention and thoughts mollify.
I hear her whisper, "It's alright."
Just as she did when we were kids.

Although she's gone,
I'm aware of her presence.
It is the little things noticed,
That make me aware she's near.

The fragrance from long ago,
Just a whiff of her perfume.
Her bracelet when I wear it,
Feels so comfortable and warm.

Although people pass,
They are not really gone.
They hover and gently let us know,
They are present, just out of our sight.

(Written in memory of my sister, Linda Antonelli, 1941-1962.)

THEY TAKE MY BREATH AWAY

Mean people suck the air out of life,
Without caring whether you live or die.
They think they deserve another breath,
Maybe they just used their last share of air.

I keep staring to see if they start to turn blue.
That's what a lack of oxygen will clearly do.
Mean people lack self-esteem,
Because they spend their time just being mean.

Maybe, if they stopped being so mean,
They'd find their real purpose on earth.
Bringing happiness and love to all,
With a result of blessings from everyone.

TRUST AND LUST

We begin to trust,
Then fall in lust.
Wondering what's next
To enjoy.

The friendship begins,
Its long path to the summit,
To reach the top,
Of a long awaited high.

You have gained the trust,
And enjoyed the lust.
But the mountain climbed,
Is about to crumble.

You fell out of lust,
And trust,
The mountain has crumbled.
Begin again the climb to the summit.

Lee Christine Brownlee

Your Embrace

You embrace me and it releases all sadness,
Your touch and gentle whispers capture my heart,
And leave me longing for more.
When I awaken from my dreamy state,
I reach for your embrace,
Searching through my sleepy slumber,
To find I have been alone in your dreamy embrace.

EMOTIONAL ME

My mind wanders, my emotions run high,
I'm in deep search of that special guy,
But where to look, how to find him,
Especially how to select, and why?

What does it take to decide the particulars,
Who should go, and who should stay?
Is there a way of knowing,
Who's lying, and who's a fake?

You want someone kind, considerate,
And thoughtful, but how do you know,
Which one will be faithful,
And which one will falter?

He must be kind,
And above all intelligent,
But his intellectual curiosity
Must not be a bore.

Above all his love,
Must be never-ending,
His generosity noticeable,
And hopefully plentiful.

Helping in the kitchen,
And around the house.
Making that happy nest,
For his family and wife.

Lee Christine Brownlee

All this must not exceed,
His thoughtfulness, and remembrance.
What more attributes should he possess,
In order to win my heart?

Now with all these qualities,
And courtesies,
What are his wants
And needs of me?

Will I be acceptable and return his love,
Generosity, and understanding,
Or is this that one-way street
I keep hearing about?

Can we be what we expect of our mate,
Can we perform without error of fate?
Will we disappoint our best friend for life?
With our unthoughtful actions and unkind distrust?

CHANGE

The city has changed,
Perception askew.
Excitement I felt as a kid,
No longer holds true.

Busy people hustling about,
Places to go and people to view.
Strangers I'll never see again,
Wondering if they are feeling okay.

Today the tired eyes with furrowed brows,
Worrisome glances are tossed about.
Others just lingering with nothing to do,
Or have they just lost their way in life too.

I miss the people who excited my day,
Newspaper peddlers with the latest edition.
People on buses grabbing seats, holding on tight.
This could be the ride of their life.

The whole family waiting at home,
For the day's events to unfold.
Although home has changed,
The family is off doing their thing.

The buildings are taller,
The streets more crowded.
People are shoving,
And times aren't funny.

Lee Christine Brownlee

Politeness replaced,
With much sarcasm and hate.
No good evening,
To people in passing.

That evening stroll with,
Your family after dinner,
Has been replaced with,
A video clip from your neighbor.

Can't make it to the kids,
Sporting events.
Life's too busy,
We'll have to record it instead.

Say your prayers,
And tuck yourself in bed.
We're watching,
The football game instead.

Take a step back in time,
And remember the events.
Things that made us smile,
And life worthwhile.

Remember the quality,
Time with the ones you loved?
The ones you went home to,
And greeted with a hug.

You'd reach to open a building door
You'd hear a voice say, "After you, ma'am."
Today you reach for the door,
And the man behind you squeezes past you to be first.

You get on the subway
And go for a seat.
But the young man standing next to you,
Thinks it is his seat.

The lack of manners is frightening,
And friendliness has come to a halt.
Where is that world of happy faces?
So much meanness and rudeness from all.

Lee Christine Brownlee

SENTENCED

Loved,
And, lost you.
I'm sentenced to life,
Without you.

TETHERED TO THIS WORLD

I long for years gone by…
Dreamed of happier times.
Memories I hold,
That tether me to this world.

Longing for love,
Or all the loves long gone.
How strong is this tether,
That connects me to this world?

I do not know,
But I will hold on tight.
Till I can hold on no more,
Then I'll let go.

After holding on tight.
To the happier times of life,
Tethered to this world,
Was sheer delight.

Lee Christine Brownlee

TIME FLIES

Time passes so quickly,
Where does it reside?
Is it in the clouds above us,
Or simply passing by?

Does it really gain speed,
As we grow older?
Passing more quickly,
Then it did when we were young?

Do we really lose time,
When we're stuck in traffic?
And if we lose time,
Does someone find it?

What makes it appear to speed up,
And then slow down when we're bored?
How can it be controlled,
When we want to dwell on thoughts?

Why must we mark time,
As it passes us by?
Or pick up our pace,
When time flies?

Whose idea was it anyway,
To fritter our time away?
Save certain things to do,
When we have more time to spare?

If we didn't have time,
Would things not pass us by?
Would we finish to-do lists,
More efficiently than before?

Does time appear to fly by,
As we get older?
Only because we start,
Moving slower?

Why must the minutes tick away,
As if they were lost forever and a day?
Do we really get back that hour lost,
When Daylight Savings Time starts?

Is there a big time clock in the heavens,
We'll use when it's time to clock out?
Or will we run out of time,
And time will just stop?

Lee Christine Brownlee

SUICIDE IS SILLY

Suicidal tendencies are below the surface,
Despite the happy days that surround our focus.
Those drowning feelings that torment our soul,
When we're teetering on the edge of that big black hole.

Swallow the pills and secretly say goodbyes,
Knowing the pain will not survive.
Feel yourself drifting off to sleep,
Thinking... At last at peace.

Somehow hours swiftly pass,
You awaken in a fright.
This can't be true as I'm still alive,
What went wrong with my plan last night?

Must explore my purpose on earth,
Struggle to understand why it didn't work.
Selfish to try and hurt so many,
Because of giving up on life's journey.

Prepare and repair life today,
Discover what the escape was from.
Fulfill the hopes and dreams once had,
So happiness for many can be planned.

But what if you don't awaken?
What happens to those forsaken?
Who will be there to help them,
Along life's rocky path?

How selfish is one,
To leave so many behind,
Those who needed the guidance,
Along life's rocky land.

INNOCENT DRINK

Wonder why people drink?
Looking to make more friends,
Maybe even relax a bit,
Then find they cannot think.

Maybe at first they're too uptight,
Then think a drink just might,
Relax them enough to win that plight,
What a wobbly-wobbly sight.

They take that drink and then another,
Wobbling to and fro.
How many promises were made,
For what and who will be forsaken?

Drink is just the tell-all-liquid
Tells some they're a bore,
Tells others the real score,
But doesn't tell who they really are.

Days and Nights

Restless days and sleepless nights,
Too many without a fight.
Who is there to complain to,
And who is there to give me advice?

I convince myself I'm always right,
But who corrects me when I'm not.
Daylight fades to darkness,
And daily noises fade to silence.

Cooking for one is not fun,
Eating alone is all I've done.
Cleaning our home takes time,
Especially when the mess is mine.

The quiet turns the house too cold.
The loneliness does not keep me warm.
I wonder what will become of me,
Without you to fill my needs.

Lee Christine Brownlee

LAUGHING IN THE RAIN

Laughing in the rain.
Walking on the beach,
Hearing the echo,
Of your own laughter.

Skipping stones.
Mellowing tones.
Recapturing moments,
Of times gone by.

Dwelling on sounds.
Hearing their rapture,
Answering their call,
Responding to life.

You hear a ringing.
It is you calling.
Reminiscing of times.
Alone in your thoughts.

Easing the stress,
Responding to life.
Meld into rest,
Erasing all pain.

Remembering laughter,
Recapturing time.
Slipping into slumber,
For the very last time.

Rings in a Tree

Miss you more than I thought possible.
More than should be allowed.
Miss your humor and your laughter.
The way you loved me forever after.

The years ticked by and decades appeared,
Like the rings in a tree, growing wider each year.
Tick-Tock, Tick-Tock, another ring in the tree,
Tick-Tock...Tock...Tock...
Gone, like the time on a clock.

Lee Christine Brownlee

Who Am I to Care?

What is it that makes me care,
But who am I to dare?
My lonely heart just breaks,
But who am I to care?

Your gentle touch moved my emotions,
Led me to explore,
The time that's passed and longing space,
It's in my heart that breaks.

I know you've passed and left my life,
But in my heart you'll stay.
In my heart that longing space,
Will always be your place.

The years have passed,
Fading memories of our time,
But my heart knows I dare,
Because I am the one who cares.

Unaltered Memories

My mind wanders,
Thinking of the could have beens,
And should have beens;
But mainly the memories of what was.

I regress trying to imagine,
An altered view of life,
An image enlightenment,
A surprising twist.

I return to reality,
Discovering wonderful images,
Of an unaltered life of happiness,
And unforgettable memories of you.

Lee Christine Brownlee

STORMY WEATHER
(ODE TO STORM SANDY)

Winter storms and howling winds,
Cutting paths to clear its way.
Angry ocean waves crashing on shore,
Crumbling structures along its path.

Wonder where this storm began,
Bringing destruction to our land.
It's cruel and treacherous ways,
Cause havoc as it destroys its prey.

Hope this storm passes without harming,
Those who stumble without warning.
Angry winds and continued rains,
Frighten those who dare to remain.

The rain and lightning cloud the wind,
While its angry attack is secretly tracked.
Marked for reference of future paths,
Comes sunny days begging forgiveness of the attack.

Faces of whose lives are touched,
Show sorrow and pain that can't be stirred.
Sallow looks and anguished fears,
Subside over time as we revere.

Seeing tears and hearing cries,
Of people sobbing for those who died.
Leave watchers praying for those whose loss,
Is more than any possession could cost.

Trees and leaves once were full,
Colors glistened under the dew.
The storm has blown the trees all bare,
Leaving jagged branches and leafless stare.

We clean and renew our land to begin again,
Preparing for another angry wind.
Nature will again attack its prey,
And renew its strength to storm again one day.

Shattered lives and homes destroyed,
Weathered and flooded on ravaged land.
Will again be renewed and life reborn,
As the living prepare for the next big storm.

(Ode to Storm Sandy written while the storm was passing through
Arlington, Virginia, on its way North, up the Atlantic Coast)

Challenges

Your quest each morning when you awake,
Is to face new challenges,
You may have that day.

Enable your inner strength to take over,
And awaken your body,
To each movement it makes.

Dancing through life,
And facing new goals,
Enriches your life and those that you love.

The support from your family and friends,
Sparks new energy into those tired limbs,
By adding rhythm to every step you take.

Dancing and singing,
Feeling the beat,
And staying instep,
With the sounds that you hear.

My Angel My Hero,
Is with you each day,
Encouraging every step,
On your dance floor of life.

(Written as an encouragement for people with Parkinson's disease and the struggles they face every day. My Angel My Hero is their support group.)

SUMMER IS GONE

Windy mornings and rainy nights,
With a dash of sunlight in the middle.
Hazy, lazy Sundays,
Mark the arrival of Winter.

Swirling leaves on the ground,
Blended with dust particles in the air,
Creating visual havoc,
Squinting to see where I'm going.

Shorter days appear to have less light,
Surrounded by more hours of darkness,
Taunt my mind.
Speckled with dreary rain drizzling,
Down through filtered light.

Reminds me of childhood days,
Gazing out my bedroom window.
Daydreaming of sunny trails,
Whistling birds and huge dragonflies,
Fluttering about.

Those days seem so distant in my mind,
As the shadow of winter hovers overhead.
Covering my days like a thick foggy blanket,
Of dismal distant sunlight.
Awaiting a tiny sliver of ray to peek through.

Lee Christine Brownlee

QUINTESSENTIAL

In our busy lives do we allow ourselves,
The quiescent moments to reflect,
That extra slumberous morning of rest,
While reflecting on beauty in our life?

Have we allowed those precious sunlit days,
To escape without a moment's notice in time.
Or captured the essence of time passing,
While pondering the minutes quickly slipping away.

There is no reversal of time or sunlit morning reruns.
Recapturing thoughts and remembrance of moments.
Halcyon days of youthful experiences and joyous times.
Dreams and goals appeared easy and achievable,
And we were driven by the future before us.

Kicking those dreams and goals to the sidelines,
And letting them crumble and turn to dust.
Awaken those memories, recapture the dreams,
Enjoy their energy and relight the sunlit mornings.
The energy rests in the quiescent moments of reflection.

Enjoy the relaxation and drifting off to sleep,
Remembering streams of light and morning dew.
Dancing raindrops on windowsills.
Laughter that seemed it would never end.
Childhood friends that never tired of playing.

Recall memorable times,
Allow the thoughts to linger as your mind drifts.
Recalling those happy days,
Quintessential days of our life.

TOGETHER

I want to laugh till it hurts,
And never cry again.
Smile till my cheeks ache,
Looking at you sleep.

Dance till I can't stand up anymore,
And treasure our time,
Till the clock stops ticking.

To dream that endless dream,
Experiencing time before my eyes,
And wake up with you next to me,
Smiling in your sleep.

I want to share my waking moments,
With you next to me,
While we grow old together,
Laugh and smile together
Sharing our lives,
Forever in my dreams.

It's Not You, It's Me

I thought our love was over,
Then suddenly, I fell in love with you,
All over again.

I felt the thrill and excitement,
Of new love before me.
With the old comfortable feel,
Of having you near me.

The difference in me, now,
Was to stop looking at my feelings.
And consider your emotions, instead.
And when I did that, I knew,
That I clearly loved you.

It's not you,
It's me.

Lee Christine Brownlee

"Retake" Please!

I'd like a retake on my life.
I'm not happy with the way it turned out.
Maybe just a few minor changes,
To the plot and script will do the trick.

Let's cut out a couple of the actors,
They're acting wasn't that good,
And they overplayed their parts.
I think we should possibly cut them out too.

A few odd characters stumbled in,
Aggressively ruined the plot.
I think they should be eliminated,
From the script and walk-on parts.

I'll select the characters I want,
And when they should appear,
What they should say,
And how they should behave,
And I'll tell them when to cheer.

There are a few chapters
That must not be overlooked.
You will know them as I'm smiling
Throughout each scene from ear-to-ear.

But let's cut out all the crying scenes,
It only makes me feel sad,
And eliminate all the people,
Who brought on the fear and tears.

Let me know when you've done the editing,
I'll review it in my dreams.
Then we'll splice in some more happy scenes,
They're the best of all my dreams.

If you hear any yelling,
I want that cut out too.
This will be the final run,
As I'm running out of film to cut.

Oh Hell, fire the original cast,
I'll hold new auditions in the morning.
Tell them to just wear a smile,
And they've got the part.

Lee Christine Brownlee

MEANDERING MEADOWS

Meandering down a country path,
Touching and smelling each flower I pass,
Brings back memories of faded fragrances missed,
Along life's path of sunlit mist.

Even the weeds in meadows are beautiful,
They flower and spread beauty just like the rest.
Even the weeds are kissed by the sun,
Drizzled on with raindrops from above.

Petals so soft and delicate,
That bruise when touched just like a rose.
Their colors are vibrant and rich,
Colors of golds, pinks, reds, and blues.
Staying moist until they are picked.

Collecting an armful of weeds and wild flowers,
Hugging them to my chest,
Giving them the same tender affection,
Renews their fragrance when touched.

The moist earth clings to the roots,
As each flowering stem is tugged from the earth.
Clinging to each stem unbruised flowers.
Looking down at their place in the ground.
Where raindrops once fell.

Meandering through the richness and beauty,
Each color different from the rest.
Hugging all this beauty,
Restores life to every petal.

I stop and reflect on life while collecting my thoughts,
Are the petals not like people.
Of family and friends nearby?
When a life is touched by love from a friend,
Does that life not become enriched with beauty?

I hold someone I care about in my arms,
Hug that person to my chest,
Watch that person come back to life,
Like the flowers picked in the meadows loved.

Lee Christine Brownlee

CPSIA information can be obtained at www.ICGtesting.com
Printed in the USA
BVOW06s0527110816

458698BV00001B/1/P